Writing Without Boundaries

What's Possible When
Students Combine Genres

Suzette Youngs

and

Diane Barone

HEINEMANN
Portsmouth, NH

KH

Heinemann
A division of Reed Elsevier Inc.
361 Hanover Street
Portsmouth, NH 03801–3912
www.heinemann.com

Offices and agents throughout the world

Library of Congress Cataloging-in-Publication Data
Youngs, Suzette.
    Writing without boundaries : what's possible when students combine genres / Suzette Youngs and Diane Barone.
        p. cm.
    Includes bibliographical references and index.
    ISBN-13: 978-0-325-01041-0 (alk. paper)
    ISBN-10: 0-325-01041-2
    1. English language—Composition and exercises—Study and teaching (Elementary). 2. Language arts (Elementary). 3. Literary form—Study and teaching (Elementary).   I. Barone, Diane M.   II. Title.
LB1576.Y64 2007
372.62'3—dc22   2007001636

Editor: Tom Newkirk
Production editor: Sonja S. Chapman
Cover design: Night & Day Design
Compositor: Reuben Kantor, QEP Design
Manufacturing: Steve Bernier

Printed in the United States of America on acid-free paper
11 10 09 08 07   ML   1   2   3   4   5

7/29/08

Contents

Acknowledgments

We want to thank Ali Gamble and Lisa Banes, two incredible fifth- and sixth-grade teachers. You both opened the doors to your classrooms and shared your most candid thoughts about writing with us. We appreciate your dedication as you help your students become talented writers. We also want to thank our past students whose work we have used throughout this book. Your writing samples give voice and vision to our writing.

We want to say thank you to Tom Romano, the father of multigenre writing. Your books and presentations have been an inspiration to us for many years. Thank you, Lois Bridges, for believing in this book from the beginning, and thank you, Tom Newkirk, for seeing us through to the end. Thank you, Pat G. Smith, for sharing your interest in multigenre writing so many years ago. Our discussions made a difference for many young writers.

Suzette would like to thank her husband, Kevin, and her daughters, Chandler and Morgan, for their love and support throughout the writing of this book; her mom for being her eternal cheerleader; and her brother Frank, who has opened many doors.

CHAPTER 1

Introduction to Genre and Multigenre Writing

TEACHER: What is multigenre writing?

TY: The multigenre writing project is a four-piece set with two larger pieces and two shorter pieces and you get to pick whatever genres there might be to fit your topic and my topic is basketball legends, so I made an interview, which is a genre, a calendar, a poster, and a newspaper article.

ANNA: Take different genres and put them together in a topic. They need to work with the topic.

TENEKA: You need to build a schema for your topic, you need to do research—you need to research each genre so that it will seem authentic.

KATIE: You want people to recognize the genre.

As seen in this small segment of student dialogue, these students understood multigenre writing as a complex writing effort in which they chose different genres to investigate a topic. They carefully considered perspective, audience, and the purpose for each genre. Each genre selection added an element not present in the others. What is amazing about the preceding conversation is that the participants were elementary students, not high school students. They clearly had knowledge of a wide range of genres and how to select the most appropriate ones to deliver their message.

In addition to this brief discussion of multigenre writing, we have provided an example of a completed project to help you better understand the strengths and complexities of such a project. Figure 1.1 displays samples from each selection of a completed multigenre writing project that Emily created after researching Sir Ernest Shackleton.

Through perusing this sample, it will become clear that Emily thoroughly understood her topic and was able to share it in very flexible ways such as a riddle, a letter to Shackleton's wife and a letter to the queen of England, a speech, a want ad, and an alphabet book. She also assumed the writing style of each author and used words and phrases reflecting the time period of Shackleton.

So What Exactly Is Multigenre Writing?

Romano described multigenre writing to his students in this way:

A multigenre paper arises from research, experience, and imagination. It is not an uninterrupted, expository monolog nor a seamless narrative nor a

FIGURE 1.1
Samples of Emily's Multigenre Project

Who Am I?

I sailed across the Arctic in a boat I called my own,
And throughout the world a hero I am known,
I manned our ship until it sunk in the ice,
We had to give our dogs for a sacrifice....

Dear Emily,

I miss you terribly. It's very cold here but every time I think of you it warms my heart. I'm beginning to get sick and I am afraid we will have to retreat....

Your husband,

Ernest

Your royal highness, Queen Elizabeth,

I wholeheartedly thank you for knighting me Sir Ernest Shackleton. I believe that I was worthy and hope you trust the same. I would have you to high tea and humbly thank you face to face but that would be impossible since I am on a ship in the Arctic yet again....

Sincerely,

Sir Ernest Shackleton

Speech

CREW WANTED FOR HAZARDOUS JOURNEY, SMALL WAGES, BITTER COLD, LONG MONTHS OF COMPLETE DARKNESS, CONSTANT DANGER, SAFE RETURN DOUBTFUL.... Would you accept this? No, not many would, but there were a few good men and myself who did.

I was born Ernest Henry Shackleton in Ireland in 1874; the same year my parents Edward and Alexandra's potato crop failed. I was not expected to live through the year but I did—that's when I showed my first sign of the strength that would lead to my career.

When I was six my father finished med school and we moved to England where he was a doctor and I attended grade school. I found it boring, but I loved to read and had a vivid imagination. By the time I attended secondary school called Dulwich College, I was enjoying education and they described me as an odd boy, the adventurous type. Reading *20,000 Leagues Under the Sea* made me long to go to the sea myself and although my father hoped I would follow in his footsteps he agreed to let me set sail. So I quit school and worked as a merchant marine quickly advancing through the ranks till I was qualified to command any British ship....

Rebuttal

Most people, finding themselves helplessly adrift on ice at the end of the earth, would simply give up; not I.... People say I inspired men with calm confidence, unfailing optimism, and selfless leadership so we all could survive and be better for our hardships. Fellow polar explorer Roald Admunsen said of me, "I know of no better example then what that man has accomplished."

CREW WANTED FOR HAZARDOUS JOURNEY TO THE ARTIC

Small wages, bitter cold, long months of complete darkness, constant danger, horrible weather, small variety of foods, frostbite likely, lack of fresh food, hard work necessary, horrible homesickness, safe return doubtful.

Sissies need not apply.

Sir Ernest Shackleton

FIGURE 1.1
(continued)

Ernest Shackleton's Alphabet Book

A is for Arctic where I sailed.

B is for brothers, how I treated my men.

C is for courage that you had to have.

D is for deadly voyage that I took.

E is for Elephant Island where we stayed.

F is for friendly, which I was to my crew....

collection of poems. A multigenre paper is composed of many genres and subgenres, each piece self-contained, making a point of its own yet connected by themes or topic and sometimes by language, images, and content. In addition to many genres, a multigenre paper may also contain many voices, not just the author's. The trick is to make such a paper hang together. (2000, x–xi)

Romano's work on multigenre writing has typically focused on high school and college writers. Not surprisingly, much of his description of multigenre writing centered on research papers in which students used a variety of genres to explain and describe a topic. The strength of these papers was that students combined numerous sources and forms of writing to enrich and deepen the content of their reports.

Camille Allen (2001) extended the work of Romano to elementary students. Both Allen and Romano nudge teachers to engage students in writing that is based on one topic or theme. Students are expected to create multiple pieces of writing through a variety of genres. As students write multigenre pieces they broaden the boundaries of genre as they blend genres and create hybrid genres.

Pragmatically, multigenre writing is just another genre of writing that is included during regular writing time. Students learn about various genres in reading and writing, and multigenre writing serves as a vehicle with which they can explore combinations of genres and how they make unique contributions to a whole project. For example, students learn that a list of different kinds of bats provides one piece of information; a poem about bats, another; and an informational report in which bats are compared, yet another perspective. Each part contributes to a more thorough knowledge about bats.

So What Is Important to Know About Genres?

Kress (1993) suggests that genre is a social process and the purpose of genre should be taken into consideration when teaching students. He recommends that students be exposed to a wide variety of genres, especially those that are pervasive outside classroom walls. He believes that if these familiar genres are acknowledged in school, perhaps children will be more successful in literacy achievement and understanding. For instance, students may be very familiar with list making, completing forms, and so on—typical literacy behaviors conducted at home. By making these genres legitimate in school, teachers help students see that home literacies are valued at school, thus creating a closer link between home and school literacy.

Unlike the recommendations of Kress, many teachers, especially of primary-grade students, value narrative over informational text. In Duke's classic study (2000), few minutes were ever set aside for the exploration of informational text in the primary grades. She wondered how students would learn to read and appreciate this broad genre if they never were exposed to it.

Complementary to Duke's research, many studies (Chapman 1999; Donovan 2001; Donovan and Smolkin 2002; Kamberelis 1999) have compared informational and narrative knowledge of students in the elementary setting. Overall, they found that even at an early age, children were aware and had the ability to use narrative structure. However, their familiarity with informational text was not as developed. These studies investigated the developmental process of genre awareness. Not surprisingly, the overall recommendation from these studies was that students need to be exposed to many other genres besides narrative in the primary grades (Caswell and Duke 1998).

This research leads to two expansive ways to view text—narrative and expository. While these categories lead to a binary division of literature, they do not highlight the great variety among the forms within each category. For instance, narrative can be further divided as follows (this list is not meant to be exhaustive):

❖ poetry

❖ mursery rhyme

❖ songbook

❖ play

❖ picture storybook

❖ wordless book

❖ myth

❖ legend

❖ tall tale

❖ folktale

❖ fable

❖ fantasy

❖ science fiction

❖ mystery

❖ horror

❖ realistic fiction

❖ historical fiction

In a similar way, expository text can be further separated:

❖ biography

❖ persuasive

❖ descriptive

- ❖ informational text
  - ▪ science
  - ▪ social studies
  - ▪ health
  - ▪ art
  - ▪ sports
- ❖ reference text
- ❖ dictionary
- ❖ thesaurus
- ❖ map
- ❖ newspaper

Additionally, each of these broad types of text can be separated by its organizational structure. For example, narrative text can be written using flashbacks, from multiple perspectives, and so on. Expository text can be organized as description, cause and effect, comparison, a time line, and so on. In their exploration of genre, students learn about text organization as well as categories of genre.

Multigenre writing allows students to include the previously listed genres and to extend the lists with many others. Figure 1.2 highlights several additional genres.

It would be simplistic to believe that all text neatly falls into a broad or more specific category of genre. For example, books like *The Jolly Postman* (Ahlberg and Ahlberg 2001) and the Magic School Bus series (Cole) blur genres. In *The Jolly Postman,* there is a narrative structure that is interrupted with letters, invitations, and lists. It is a powerful text because the authors have a deep understanding of many

ABC book	comic strip	gossip column	pop-up book
about the author page	commercial	how-to manual	propaganda
adventure story	crash site report	instructions	poster
advertisement	death certificate	inventory	radio report
advice column	death notice	invitation	recipe
animal book	diary entry	invoice	report card
anthology	diploma	lesson plan	riddle
autobiography	document	letter	script
banner	drawing	magazine article	song
battle plans	encyclopedia	marriage certificate	speech
board game	entry	medical record	summary
book review	epitaph	memoir	thank-you note
brochure	eulogy	model	time line
bumper sticker	family tree	newsletter	tombstone
calendar	fairy tale	newspaper	trivia
cartoon	floor plan	photo with caption	videotape
children's picture	flyer	pin (e.g., politcal slogan	weather report
book	greeting card	on a pin)	web page
collage of poetry/lines	grocery list	political cartoon	yearbook

FIGURE 1.2
Possible Genres

genres and therefore are able to stretch the boundaries of narrative structure. This text is an example of the possibilities for all children in classrooms—to have knowledge of genres in such a deep way that they stretch their boundaries.

So How Should Teachers Teach About Genre and Multigenre Writing?

Calkins (1994) and Wood Ray (2001) advocate teaching children to write through genres. Each proposes teaching writing with explicit instruction about a genre. They see the connections between text and modeling that text structure in writing. As children become familiar with and knowledgeable about a particular genre, they are able to create a writing piece of their own adhering to particular traits of that genre as defined by a mentor or model texts (Wood Ray 2001). Some genre theorists (Christie, 1993; Cope and Kalantzis 1993a, b, c; Delpit 1995; Kress 1993, 1999; Luke 1993) have claimed that children need to have explicit instruction to understand what genre is and how it works. This knowledge, they believe, is fundamental for students before they can push the boundaries of genre. For instance, a teacher might support students in learning to write a poem that identifies facts about a state as an introduction to poetry.

Responding to the importance of explicitness, we have included descriptions and examples throughout this book to support instruction of multigenre writing. Clearly, this form, similar to other forms of writing, is not something that students can intuit. There needs to be modeling and direct instruction as to the structure of possible genres and on how to write such genres with support before students can be successful independently.

How Will This Book Help My Students with Multigenre Writing?

Writing Without Boundaries: What's Possible When Students Combine Genres is organized into seven chapters. They can support a teacher as he embarks on a multigenre experience. Chapter 2 establishes the classroom organization that is necessary to successfully engage in multigenre writing. It assists teachers in sharing literature with students to build knowledge and understanding of genres. Chapter 3 provides a practical step-by-step process for beginning a multigenre project. A full project overview is shared along with templates of forms to support student writing.

Chapter 4 builds on the previous chapters and offers more detail about teaching and managing multigenre writing projects. For instance, we share details about genre investigations. We provide small-group and whole-class lessons. The chapter ends with suggestions for conferring with students to enrich the writing they have produced in early drafts.

Chapter 5 provides examples from intermediate and primary grades. It offers an opportunity to see the richness of multigenre studies. Chapter 6 provides support for how multigenre projects target large-scale assessments and standards. It provides a multitude of ways to assess student multigenre projects and showcases ways to publish and celebrate student work. Technology links are provided as well.

Finally, Chapter 7 takes a brief look at questions teachers have about multigenre writing. All of the chapters in this book are pragmatically structured. This is a book where teachers can find all of the necessary details to be successful with multigenre writing.

Closing Thoughts

From this brief overview, it is easy to see the multiple possibilities for students to explore genres, if given the opportunity. We believe that multigenre writing allows for this important exploration. It encourages writers to find their own voice and culturally meet their needs and expectations as they choose and define appropriate genres for their writing projects (Romano 1995). It allows them to bridge genres that are typically used either inside or outside of school. It also encourages students to decide the importance of particular genres in building their collections of evidence in multigenre writing.

Teachers can stretch the boundaries even more by using multigenre writing (Romano 1995, 2000) to bridge the theoretical gap between process writing (Graves 1994; Calkins 1994; Fletcher 2001; Wood Ray 2001) and genre pedagogy (Cope and Kalantzis 1993b). It widens the scope of reading and writing possibilities for writers in elementary classrooms.

References

Ahlberg, J., and A. Ahlberg. 2001. *The Jolly Postman, or Other People's Letters.* New York: Little, Brown

Allen, C. A. 2001. *The Multigenre Research Paper: Voice, Passion and Discovery in Grades 4–6.* Portsmouth, NH: Heinemann.

Calkins, L. M. 1994. *The Art of Teaching Writing.* Portsmouth, NH: Heinemann.

Caswell, L. J., and N. K. Duke. 1998. "Non-narrative as a Catalyst for Literacy Development." *Language Arts* 75, 108–117.

Chapman, M. 1999. "Situated, Social, Active: Rewriting Genre in the Elementary Classroom." *Written Communication* 16 (4): 469–90.

Christie, F. 1993. "Curriculum Genres: Planning for Effective Teaching." In *The Powers of Literacy: A Genre Approach to Teaching Writing,* ed. B. Cope and M. Kalantzis, 154–78. Pittsburgh: University of Pittsburgh Press.

Cole, J. The Magic School Bus Series. New York: Scholastic.

Cope, B., and M. Kalantzis. 1993a. "Histories of Pedagogy, Cultures of Schooling." In *The Powers of Literacy: A Genre Approach to Teaching Writing,* ed. B. Cope and M. Kalantzis, 38–62. Pittsburgh: University of Pittsburgh Press.

———. 1993b. "Introduction: How a Genre Approach to Literacy Can Transform the Way Writing Is Taught." In *The Powers of Literacy: A Genre Approach to Teaching Writing,* ed. B. Cope and M. Kalantzis, 1–21. Pittsburgh: University of Pittsburgh Press.

———. 1993c. "The Power of Literacy and the Literacy of Power." In *The Powers of Literacy: A Genre Approach to Teaching Writing,* ed. B. Cope and M. Kalantzis, 63–89. Pittsburgh: University of Pittsburgh Press.

Delpit, L. 1995. *Other People's Children: Cultural Conflict in the Classroom.* New York: New York Press.

Donovan, C. 2001. "Children's Development and Control of Written Story and Informational Genres: Insights from One Elementary School." *Research in the Teaching of English* 35: 394–447.

Donovan, C., and L. B. Smolkin. 2002. Children's Genre Knowledge: An Examination of K–5 Students' Performance on Multiple Tasks Providing Differing Levels of Scaffolding. *Reading Research Quarterly* 37: 428–65.

Duke, N. K. 2000. "3.6 Minutes per Day: The Scarcity of Informational Texts in First Grade." *Reading Research Quarterly* 35: 202–24.

Fletcher, R. 2001. *The Writing Workshop: The Essential Guide.* Portsmouth, NH: Heinemann.

Graves, D. 1994. *A Fresh Look at Writing.* Portsmouth, NH: Heinemann.

Kamberelis, G. 1999. "Genre Development and Learning: Children Writing Stories, Science Reports, and Poems." *Research in the Teaching of English* 33: 403–60.

Kress, G. 1993. "Genre as Social Process." In *The Powers of Literacy: A Genre Approach to Teaching Writing,* ed. B. Cope and M. Kalantzis, 22–37. Pittsburgh: University of Pittsburgh Press.

———. 1999. "Genre and the Changing Contexts for English Language Arts." *Language Arts* 76 (6): 461–69.

Luke, A. 1993. Introduction. In *The Powers of Literacy: A Genre Approach to Teaching Writing,* ed. B. Cope and M. Kalantzis, vii–viii. Pittsburgh: University of Pittsburgh Press.

Romano, T. 1995. *Writing with Passion: Life Stories, Multiple Genres.* Portsmouth, NH: Boynton/Cook, Heinemann.

———. 2000. *Blending Genre, Altering Style: Writing Multigenre Papers.* Portsmouth, NH: Boynton/Cook.

Wood Ray, K. 2001. *The Writing Workshop: Working Through the Hard Parts (And They're All Hard Parts).* Urbana, IL: NCTE.

CHAPTER 2

Before Multigenre Writing . . . Establishing the Writing Workshop and Knowledge of Genre

Genre is like a piece of writing that you're thinking about and then you put all your thoughts into one topic, that's a genre. I decided to do a tombstone because I thought it would go good with wrestling legends, the wrestlers that don't wrestle any more. Then I did a banner because I thought it would be good to put like two good wrestlers in a fight so people would be more interested. I made two pictures of them so you could see how they look and who they are and put their name right under their picture and that is how I did it.

In this quote, Juan was talking to his teacher about the decisions he made in selecting genres for his project on wrestlers. Juan was able to share his purposeful decisions on the genres he would use. He was also aware of what his audience might understand about his choices, and he planned to carefully tailor his banner, in this case, to make it more interesting and appealing. Conversations like Juan's do not just magically happen one day. To initiate such conversation, teachers must understand complex classroom organization and have knowledge about writing and genres.

This chapter provides the underpinnings for successful writing, particularly successful multigenre writing. We begin with an overview of a writing workshop organization and then move to strategies to support students' awareness of genres.

Beginning the Writing Workshop

Writing workshop should start on the first day of school. While some of your students will have been in classrooms with a daily writing workshop, many won't have. Lately, we have found that fewer children than in the past have participated in writing workshop. They have experienced assessment writing, journal writing, and writing about what they are reading, although they typically respond to questions. This writing infrequently moves through the writing process and it is often not a daily part of instruction. We have observed that in many schools, assessment writing practice consumes the curriculum in grades where state writing tests are administered.

Rather than assuming previous experience, it's best to start the year with all students learning about the expectations of a writing workshop. We suggest beginning by sharing *If You Were a Writer* (Nixon 1988). In this book, Melia chats with her mother about writing (her mother is a writer). Melia's mother tells her, "A writer works with words" (unnumbered). In another conversation, they explore how to write a story. Her mother explains that she "shows what is happening" (unnumbered). Later in the book the reader shares in Melia's creation of a story.

During the first week of school, the teacher and students examine this book and enter into conversation on what writers do, how they get ideas, how they begin, and other issues about writing. After having a brief discussion of this book on the first day of school, for about ten to fifteen minutes, the teacher gives each student a notebook. The kids move to their desks, if they were gathered on the floor, and they begin to pursue ideas about what they might write about in their notebooks. When students appear restless, the teacher convenes the class and students share some of their ideas. The teacher then allows a few minutes for students to record any new topics they might want to write about.

On the second day of writing workshop, the class again chats about the book. Following the discussion, students return to their notebooks. This time the teacher directs them to choose one topic and begin to write. Again, when students seem restless, the teacher gathers them and they share some of what they have written. The teacher may also engage them in discussion about the ease or difficulty they had with this first writing.

Typically, by the third or fourth day, the teacher can share the full organization of writing workshop. The focus at this point is on organization with writing in the background. Students learn that each day they will begin with a whole-class exercise. It could be exploring a book to learn about writing or as a model for writing. They may have a lesson targeting a needed skill or writing strategy. They may also discuss how the workshop is going and any changes that need to be made. Then they will have some time to write, and to close the workshop, they will come together again to share.

Structuring a Workshop

Teachers have opportunities for great variation in the way they organize a writing workshop. Some start with a lesson and others conduct the lesson at other points during the workshop. We share one way of organizing a workshop, certainly not the only way. We have found that however a workshop is organized in structure, it is important that it becomes a routine. Once students know what to expect and when, they can devote energy to writing. If they are always guessing at what comes next, they will have little energy left for writing. So routines are important for students (Calkins 1994).

As described earlier, the workshop begins with a collaborative lesson with all students in the class. The lesson is short and fast paced, typically taking about ten minutes. Then students are sent to write. Often teachers ask students to write quietly and independently for another ten minutes. This allows students to reread what they wrote the day before and to get a sense of what will be important for today's writing time. Teachers then open up the writing workshop so that students can write together, revise together, or edit together. Teachers also confer with students during this time. Teachers allocate the majority of writing workshop time to this part of the workshop. The workshop ends with about ten minutes for sharing. This sharing could be of completed pieces of writing or drafts on which students are looking for support from their peers.

Organizing for a Workshop

Teachers also create organization for storing writing and forms for supporting students. For instance, teachers decide whether students will have notebooks and/or writing folders. If the answer is yes, where will they be stored? Having them in student desks is never a great idea, as students seem to lose anything placed there. Storage is an important decision, as it allows students to know where to find and where to place their work. Teachers need to locate a consistent place for paper, pencils, rulers, staplers, and other writing supplies. Students need easy access to these materials, and they need to know the expectations for securing materials. Can they go get them anytime, or is there a specific way and time when materials need to be accessed?

If students are to revise and edit together, they will need forms to help with this process. For example, if they are to revise with another student, each of the students should write their names on a sheet so they can both confer with the teacher about this piece of writing later. The teacher might also specify on the form that they need to record the suggestions they have made for revising and why. In some situations, we have seen teachers ask students to first write a piece of text they found to be well written in another student's writing. They then write a piece of text about which they have questions. The exact wording of the form is not the critical piece. What is important is that students learn how to seriously respond to their peers and support the difficult part of writing—revision.

For editing, the teacher might also have students write their names so there is accountability. The teacher might just make copies of a list of what students are expected to edit. For instance, students might edit for capital letters, end punctuation, and five spelling errors. As students gain proficiency with editing, additional editing expectations are added. For most students, there will be no perfect final draft. They will rely on others, as professional writers do, to ensure that all editing errors are corrected.

In addition to storage, teachers reflect on how they will track students, how they will know what each student is doing. We have found one way to do this that is quite simple. We create a sheet that is organized like a calendar (see Figure 2.1). In each block we write a student's name. Then each time we confer with that student or informally observe him during writing workshop, we write a brief summary of what happened. In that way, we can track what a student is working on—what text and at which point of the process. This affords us a way to begin a conversation with the student on our next visit. We refer to the chart and ask how the task she was involved in is evolving.

Shifting Focus from Organization to Writing

When the routine is firmly in place, teachers shift their focus to student writing and helping students to see how they can improve their writing. They help students with first drafts, how to revise, and how to edit. They help students get started with writing and sustain writing over multiple days. They help students understand that first drafts are just that—there is always room for improvement through revision. They help students incorporate the ideas they have gleaned from professional writers into their work. They help writers with editing so that readers can fully appreciate

John	Micah	Juan
Working on whale report. Each page tells one fact. Remember to ask him for a synthesis at end.	Revising banner about basketball.	Editing poem about bats.

FIGURE 2.1
Student Tracking Form

what they have written. They help writers share their writing so that others can appreciate it.

In this overview of a writing workshop, several key essentials (Wood Ray, 2001) are in place to make a writing workshop successful:

1. Students are comfortable with the procedures of the writing workshop.
2. Students are knowledgeable or will become knowledgeable about exploring genre.
3. Students can articulate the strengths and needs of their writing.
4. Students write within a safe environment where they are expected to respect all writing attempts.
5. Students rely upon the consistency within the writing workshop (Calkins 1994; Fletcher and Portalupi 2001).
6. Whole- and small-group lessons are incorporated as well as individual conferences.
7. An obvious link to reading and literature can be observed.
8. A workable time line is in place for all students to work at their own pace toward publication.
9. Sharing and talking about student writing are emphasized.
10. Children write for a variety of purposes (Barone and Taylor 2006).

Importantly, the writing workshop must include time for children to write, provide a space for them to write in, and have a range of topics from which they may choose to write about (Fletcher and Portalupi 2001; Wood Ray 2001).

Beginning with a Single-Genre Study

We believe that before students can understand multiple genres, they first need to understand the essentials and purposes for a single genre. Through genre study, students understand a genre from a dual perspective—as a reader and as a writer. Isoke Nia (1999) created an outline for a writing inquiry unit genre study. Her steps included best-guess gathering, immersion, sifting, second immersion, selecting touchstone texts, touchstone try-its, writing, and reflecting and assessing.

Each of these steps helps the teacher and students define the genre for their own purposes based on the kinds of examples they bring into the classroom for closer examination. In best-guess gathering, students and teacher bring in examples of the text; then they immerse themselves as they sort and categorize the genre. Then students and teacher sift through the examples, keeping those that fit their purposes and removing those that do not fit their definition of the genre. Second immersion is a more focused immersion as they read and hear the sounds of the selected texts. Through this immersion a mentor or touchstone text emerges for the class as well as personal mentor texts for students. A *mentor text* is a book or article that will serve as the best example for a student and his writing piece. Students might base their content, structure, character, theme, or genre on the mentor text. Next, students begin to try the writing characteristics found in their mentor text. Nia described this time as a safe place to experiment with the writing within the genre. Then students begin to draft their writing piece, and finally students and teacher reflect on the product and process and assess the writing project together (Nia 1999). Nia explained that this structure would be similar for any genre study. For instance, the structure for a unit for poetry would look much the same as that for a unit on nonfiction. The following single-genre study example is similar in structure to what Nia has presented.

Connecting Reading and Writing Workshops

Once students are comfortable with writing during a workshop and understand the expectations, it is time to focus on quality texts so that students learn from master writers in the same way that art students learn from master painters and sculptors.

In order to demonstrate a single-genre study, we borrow from Suzette's classroom as she introduced a unit of study on contemporary realistic fiction that was the focus for both her reading workshop and her writing workshop. Students read and discussed books in this genre during their reading workshop time, and during their writing workshop students wrote within this genre. To launch the unit of study, Suzette began with a read-aloud of *Fly Away Home* (Bunting 1991). This book is about a boy who lives in an airport with his father. To avoid being noticed, they move from terminal to terminal. Bunting places a bird in the terminal, and when the bird flies out of the terminal it gives the boy hope that he will be able to leave and find a permanent place to live. While this book is a picture book, it contains serious material for students to explore, in particular homelessness.

Suzette read this book to her students multiple times on the first day she shared it. First she read it during reading workshop, where students could discuss the ideas and impressions they had about the book and the social implications of homelessness. This early discussion provided time for them to think about this topic and how the writer and illustrator brought it to life. They talked about the choice of an airport as the place where the father and son lived. One student thought "this was clever because there are so many people in the airport every day. No one would notice." Another student noticed the "dark colors in the book may be because this is a sad book."

Later, during writing workshop, Suzette reread the book. This time she asked students to note details in the book and characteristics that would lead to a classification of this book's genre as contemporary realistic fiction. Students offered the following characteristics for contemporary realistic fiction:

- maybe written about people the author knows
- usually written in first person
- believable characters
- characters that are like us
- characters learn to cope with their situation
- reader can learn about other cultures and issues and realistic settings

After this discussion, students continued to ponder this book, and toward the end of writing workshop they offered other characteristics:

- does not always have a happy story line or ending
- things that happen today
- serious issues
- hope for the future

At the end of the discussion, students opened their writer's notebooks and recorded what they thought was important to remember about contemporary realistic fiction.

Scattered around the room were crates filled with picture and chapter books that could be identified as contemporary realistic fiction. Students who were stuck on their own writing were invited to reread some of the classroom examples or discuss with other students what they might write about. Finally, a few students needed to draw for a bit as they gathered ideas for their personal piece of writing.

Suzette and the students selected books that would be considered contemporary realistic fiction. Students scoured these books to find additional details to help negotiate a definition of this genre.

Reading Widely Within a Genre

In order to understand a genre, students must first read widely within it as they begin to determine particular genre characteristics. For a single-genre study, students and the teacher gather many examples of text they think support their understanding of the genre. Then they read widely within the genre and note key characteristics in writing notebooks. They explore the structural features and literary elements of the genre as well as literary responses they have to this genre.

During this time in the writing workshop, students also find a mentor text that will serve as a model within the genre they would like to try. They hold on to this text and visit it often as they read and write within a genre. While there is certainly variability within a genre, a mentor text that a student loves serves as a teaching guide for learning about the genre as the child reads and models a piece of writing.

Comprehension Strategy Reading and Literature Study Groups

As children choose their mentor texts, it is important to explore how they respond to particular genres. We try to connect reading and writing workshops whenever they fit authentically. In an effort to help students understand a genre and the structures inherent within a particular genre, we utilize comprehension strategy reading groups (Serafini and Serafini Youngs 2006) and literature study groups (Peterson and Eeds 1990).

Comprehension strategy reading groups are formed to talk about particular strategies (character analysis, comparative analysis of fictional and informational text, visualizing and using background knowledge, etc.). Students need to know that strategies they use to understand poetry will be very different from those they use to understand informational text and different yet from those they use for a fairy tale. In these groups, readers of similar abilities are supported as they navigate and understand particular genre structures. As they discuss strategies they begin to understand particular features of a genre. These strategy discussions give them insights into specific features they might want to incorporate into their own writing.

In literature study groups, children respond to and discuss a variety of examples of the genre in both picture and chapter books. Understanding the kinds of literary responses certain genres elicit also provides insights into how they might want to construct a piece of writing to elicit certain personal reactions to their own text.

For example, students met in a literature discussion group that was reading *Olive's Ocean* by Kevin Henkes (2003). In this book, as Martha Boyle is getting ready to leave for a family vacation, the mother of a deceased classmate shows up at her door with a page from her daughter Olive's journal. In this journal Martha learns that Olive and she had similar dreams and aspirations to be a writer. Martha also learns that Olive thought Martha was the nicest person in her whole class while Martha never really paid any attention to her. Martha and her family spend the summer at her grandmother's home, where Martha learns a great deal about herself and her family as this new perspective changes her forever.

The group's discussion focused on character changes in Martha and how these changes drive the plotline. For instance, in the beginning of the book Martha does not want to share with her father that she dreams of becoming a writer, as he is in the throes of trying to become one himself. Martha becomes a well-developed character as her inner thoughts drive the plot and her continual battle between who she is and what she wants to be.

Then another group met that was reading *Locomotion* (Woodson 2003). This book is about an African American boy, Lonnie, who lost his parents in a fire. After their death, he and his sister were separated and placed in foster care. His sister, Lili, is adopted by a family and Lonnie must come to terms with his new foster family and school expectations of writing poetry. The entire book is written in a variety of experimental poems, as Lonnie must write poetry for a class assignment. Through this first-person account we come to know Lonnie and his struggle to accept his new situation.

In this discussion group, students talked about the serious issues of death and foster homes and how contemporary realistic fiction helps readers to see into some of these more serious issues without actually experiencing them. Frankie stated in this discussion, "On page 18 Lonnie lost his parents and I agree with Katie that it was interesting how he finally shared this information with the reader at this point. I think that he has held a lot in, even in his own personal journal." Lonnie describes his feelings and those events and characteristics he remembers about his family.

In this manner students discussed those features the author created that brought about personal reactions of empathy and understanding. In these discussions, students naturally gravitated to their own pieces and how they were trying to share something personal about their lives through the structure of contemporary realistic fiction genre.

Later, in their response logs, they wrote about their responses to the text and then ideas for writing. Frankie began to describe his character in more detail. He described what he was feeling in his story about a boy struggling to stand up to a bully. His entries were related to his literary response about the description of Lonnie's emotions. He wrote:

> Miguel is quiet now and is not talking to anyone. Antoine keeps looking at him across the playground. He just walks and does not play with anyone or he will get it from him. Miguel is scared and just wants to be left alone, he does not know how to stand up to Antoine he has too many friends on his side.

Heather, on the other hand, included a mysterious connection between two characters, mirroring the journal entry from *Olive's Ocean*. She wrote:

> There under a bush was a piece of paper. Heather picked it up. It read: top Ten People I want to Be Friends With. There on the top of the list was her name. There were other girls in the class on the list too. At the bottom of the page was the initials K.B. She knew who that was.

Finally, Lauren added more detail to her setting because she found the setting in *Olive's Ocean* to be very descriptive and vivid. She too wanted to create a memorable setting, as many settings in realistic fiction are very believable and draw the reader in. She added:

> On the coast of Oregon it is always breezy. There are green trees as far as the eye can see. The ocean is so blue and the smell is always in reach.

Negotiating the Purpose and Usefulness of a Genre

As students are in and out of strategy groups, literature study groups, and independent investigations of mentor texts, discussions in these groups and within the whole group begin to focus on the purpose and usefulness of a genre. We want students to understand that genres have purpose just by the characteristics of the piece and that genres do not exist within a vacuum. That is, people have created the names of genres and have given them power within a system of language and discourses (Luke, O'Briery, and Comber 1994). So often children are taught genre and do an investigation of it, yet do not understand when in their lives they would choose to write from this genre perspective and for what purposes. This understanding is a segue to multigenre writing, where teachers scaffold students' choices of genre so they make appropriate choices that meet the needs of their communication purposes.

Possible Age-Specific Genres	Genres That Span Age Groups
eulogy	picture book
job application	recipe
journal article	magazine article
medical record	joke book
bill	ABC book
notice of cancellation	about the author
syllabus	adventure story
crash site report	advertisement
death certificate	advice column
death notice	animal book
lesson plan	collage of poetry
invoice	

FIGURE 2.2
Age Comparison of Genres

With our example genre, contemporary realistic fiction, we investigated and researched the lives of authors to understand why they chose this genre and not another. Why do they want to tell these stories that mirror current events in children's lives rather than write an informational text about the issues or write poetry or a fantasy piece? For instance, students were surprised to learn that Eve Bunting takes special care to tell her stories. In one interview she explained that she pulled over on the side of the road in California to interview migrant farm workers so she might tell their story. She stayed overnight in a small town because she had to wait until they were done with work to speak with them. The students learned that she writes about stories that move her and gives a voice to children and their families who have not been heard before. Students learned that Eve Bunting's stories fit in the realistic fiction genre because they are based on true stories but are mixed with a touch of fiction.

We also investigate if a genre is age specific or if it spans many ages and, if so, what it looks like. With contemporary realistic fiction, Suzette's class investigated many titles for all ages and found that it did span across all ages and cultures. Other genres are geared more toward adults, like a job application and a eulogy (see Figure 2.2 for a sample of the list that class created to look at which genres related to various ages).

Interestingly, as the class investigated contemporary realistic fiction, students began to realize there were big differences between the pieces they were reading and the ones they were going to write: author age, experiences, and writing ability. Students understood that authors were adults writing about childhood issues, and they were excited to write about these issues that were happening at the moment rather than retrospectively, as most fiction writers do. They felt this perspective would give validity to their pieces, thus understanding the purpose and usefulness of the genre. For instance, Anna shared, "Being a fifth grader would be different than an adult. Things that are important to me right now might not be important to me when I am an adult. I might not include them." John shared, "My sense of humor might be different when I am older. I think a lot of things are funny now and my teacher doesn't always think so."

Students, with their teacher's guidance, also asked questions of texts: Who wrote this and why? Why does this genre exist? Who is the audience? Whose voice is heard?

It is easy to see how these questions could guide students into a critical analysis of any text. As Suzette's class investigated a genre and its characteristics, students negotiated why this genre exists in our society and discussed it as a cultural artifact. Shante shared the following in a discussion after reading *The Librarian of Basra: A True Story from Iraq* (Winter 2005): "I think *The Librarian of Basra* is a good example of how the book shows our times right now. The book is from the perspective of a librarian in Iraq. She is afraid of us [Americans] and we are supposed to be helping her have a better life."

Writing Within the Genre

After reading widely within the realistic fiction genre, students began to generate ideas for their own contemporary realistic fiction writing. Students transitioned from idea generating to working on a first draft of a realistic fiction piece. If they weren't ready for this transition, they practiced creating believable characters or settings that they might use in their pieces. Students were involved in creating drafts and conferencing with peers and the teacher about their writing ideas.

Small-Group Conferences

Once the students were comfortable in writing, Suzette gathered a small group of students together who were at the draft phase of their writing and required targeted support in creating stronger characters for their contemporary realistic fiction pieces. Rather than taking over their writing, she shared a piece that she was working on and showed them how she might think about her character and her development. On this day, she shared her story about being a first-year elementary school teacher and the humorous events that took place in that first year of teaching. Suzette read her story aloud to the group and then did a think-aloud of how she might develop a believable, funny, and caring character. When she completed the think-aloud, she asked the students for input on how she might more fully develop the main character, Miss Chalk.

When this group of students were ready to move on with their own characters, she dismissed them and convened another small group. These students did not yet have an idea for their pieces, so they worked in their writer's notebooks and looked through possible mentor texts. In this meeting, discussion focused on possible topics that they would like to try and possible formats that they would like their genre pieces to take. For instance, Michael, who is a swimmer, wanted to somehow incorporate that activity into his writing. In the ensuing discussion, the children brainstormed all the different kinds of writing pieces that a swimmer might create and possible story lines that could be created about a swimmer. Since the genre was contemporary realistic fiction, Michael wanted to base the story on some of his own experiences but change the events to what he wished would have happened . . . like winning a race.

Once the students were engaged with writing, Suzette shifted to conferring with individual students at writing conferences. For example, Keisha showed her piece and requested Suzette's help with creating a "lead that grabs the reader's attention." She also worried that her resolution was not clear enough. She had written: *I remember when I was little my grandfather would pick me up from preschool and we used to eat macaroni and cheese. My grandpa used to take me to swing on a tire swing.*

Rather than just resolve this with Keisha, Suzette asked her to bring her mentor text, *The Two of Them* by Aliki (1979). They studied how Aliki grabs the reader's attention and how she has a clear resolution. Keisha loved the way Aliki begins the story with:"The day she was born, her grandfather made her a ring of silver and a polished stone, because he loved her already. Someday it would fit her finger" (unnumbered). The session ended with Keisha talking about how her piece could be changed. When this happened, Suzette moved away and worked with another student.

Important to this conference is that Suzette placed Keisha in the lead. She referred Keisha to a mentor text and together they explored how to grab a reader's attention and to write a satisfactory resolution. While Suzette may have wanted to take over more of this revision, she knew that it was important for Keisha to develop these skills and strategies so that she could use them independently in other writing.

Practicing Within a Genre

Writing within a genre inquiry unit takes on different shapes for different students. As students investigate the genre and a mentor text, they write down ideas and practice in their writer's notebooks. They explore a genre for a while before they begin to write in that genre (Fletcher and Portalupi 2001; Nia 1999; Wood Ray 2001). An example of this experimenting is shown in Chandler's second-grade notebook (see Figure 2.3).

In this notebook entry, Chandler was trying out the voice of Beatrix Potter because her class was engaged in an in-depth investigation of Potter's work and the genre of animal fantasy. Chandler created Potter-like characters and a setting that was similar to many found in Potter's endearing stories. During the exploration time with a genre and during their response groups and strategy groups, students continually gather ideas for their pieces. As they investigate their mentor text (Nia 1999), students try out the writer's style, much like Chandler did in her Beatrix Potter fantasy piece.

We use the beginning of writing workshop to share think-alouds about writing a particular genre. During the contemporary realistic fiction unit, for instance, Suzette wrote and talked about the perspective she wanted to use. She had created a grand-

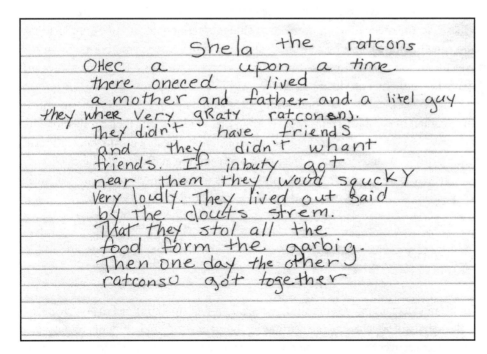

FIGURE 2.3
Chandler's Notebook Entry

mother character based on her own grandmother. She could not decide whether the story should come from a first-person journal account or from an omniscient point of view. She shared a possible opening paragraph from each perspective and students offered insights into the different tone the story would have with each perspective.

> I remember when Grandma was young and she took care of me.
>
> Her grandmother was . . .

She then turned to her mentor text, *The Sunsets of Miss Olivia Wiggins,* by Lester Laminack (1998), and read through the parts where the narrator told the story rather than Miss Olivia. She even modeled rewriting some of this text to see how it would sound.

> I sit and look at nothing and everything all at the same time. I spend much of each day just sitting. (1)

Students then practiced with different perspectives in their own notebooks to discover whose voice should be dominant in their own writing. Frankie rewrote the entry previously shown on page 16 into a first-person journal account.

> I don't want to talk to anyone now. If I stay away from Antoine then he can't get me. I wish he would quit starring at me. I am scared and just want to be left alone, I just don't know how to stand up to Antoine, and he has too many friends on his side.

This process was repeated for other genre units. First, the whole class tried creating characters for fictional pieces, or playing with language in a poetry unit, or creating a whole-class text with subheadings and bold words for an informational text study. In this way the students' actual writing of the piece became more effective and easier to complete because of all the modeling and practice that had come before.

As pieces are constructed in a new genre, the class celebrates and records on a class chart the many different forms that students' writing takes. For example, within the contemporary realistic fiction unit, students wrote picture storybooks, mysteries, adventure stories, and stories about contemporary social issues. The chart allows students to see the multitude of possibilities within a single genre.

As the class neared the completion of the contemporary realistic fiction writing, they contemplated publishing their work. Some students put their stories together and created a class book of realistic fiction while others created picture books. For this particular genre study, children their own age were the audience, so the publication was geared to getting their writing in the hands of their schoolmates and peers. The purpose and the audience drove decisions for publication.

Closing Thoughts

In this model of a single-genre study, it is evident that students need to engage in critical analysis of a genre before writing in the genre and that students should read widely to discover the purpose and usefulness of a genre. Students and teachers must negotiate the working definition of the genre because definitions blur depending on the types of examples brought into a classroom for investigation. Teachers are expected to scaffold students in their attempts to learn about, define, and use a variety of genres, and in transitioning from a close investigation of a single genre to making choices about multiple genres.

References

Aliki. 1979. *The Two of Them.* New York: Mulberry.

Barone, D., and J. Taylor. 2006. *Improving Students' Writing, K–8: From Meaning-Making to High Stakes.* Thousand Oaks, CA: Corwin.

Bunting, E. 1991. *Fly Away Home.* New York: Clarion.

Calkins, L. 1994. *The Art of Teaching Writing.* 2nd ed. Portsmouth, NH: Heinemann.

Fletcher, R., and J. Portalupi. 2001. *Writing Workshop.* Portsmouth, NH: Heinemann.

Henkes, K. 2003. *Olive's Ocean.* New York: HarperTrophy.

Laminack, L. 1998. *The Sunsets of Miss Olivia Wiggins.* Atlanta: Peachtree.

Luke, A., J. O'Brien, and B. Comber. 1994. "Making Community Texts the Objects of Study." *Australian Journal of Language and Literacy* 17 (2): 112–23.

Nia, I. 1999. "Units of Study in the Writing Workshop." *Primary Voices K–6* 8 (1), 3–12.

Nixon, J. 1988. *If You Were a Writer.* New York: Four Winds.

Peterson, R., and M. Eeds. 1990. *Grand Conversations: Literature Groups in Action.* New York: Scholastic.

Serafini, F., and S. Serafini Youngs. 2006. *Around the Reading Workshop in 180 Days.* Portsmouth, NH: Heinemann.

Winter, J. 2005. *Librarian of Basra: A True Story from Iraq.* New York: Harcourt.

Wood Ray, K. 2001. *The Writing Workshop: Working Through the Hard Parts (And They're All Hard Parts).* Urbana, IL: NCTE.

Woodson, J. 2003. *Locomotion.* New York: Penguin.

CHAPTER 3

Introducing Multigenre Writing

MARIA: Multigenre writing is the *[laughing]*.

ALLIE: Um, it's the way to get kids to *[pause]*

MARIA: I think it is a way to get them to examine and look at the way writing is actually used in our world and how they can become those kinds of writers. And it can go with any type of content area or any kind of writing you're trying to teach. Writing is something that's used in everyday life and trying to reflect the way writing is used in our everyday life.

ALLIE: They observe the genres that writers use in their books. My students now talk about genre, not just the author or illustrator.

Allie and Maria, two elementary school teachers, chatted about their use of multigenre writing. This conversation happened at the end of an academic year, when they reflected on their first foray into multigenre writing. In this brief snippet of conversation, it is obvious that they recognized important differences in their students as readers and writers. Genre had now become a focus for the teachers and their students as they read and wrote. Allie and Maria entered into their exploration of multigenre writing with each other's support. This chapter shares much of what they learned and serves as a guide for teachers as they begin their own explorations into multigenre writing.

Finding Important Topics

Before formally initiating a multigenre project, teachers ask students to consider possible topics for writing—topics that are personally meaningful to them. Typically, students search through their writer's notebooks first and simultaneously consider their hot-topic list—a list of possible writing topics in their notebooks. Within their writer's notebooks (Fletcher 2001; Wood Ray 2001), they find ideas, paragraphs, excerpts, lists of words, or beginnings of new writing pieces that they have previously recorded. Students have tried out different topics and leads and played with characteristics of genre throughout their notebooks and these serve as sources for important topics. At other times students may choose a topic inspired by a piece of writing they completed earlier in the year. For instance, Mary chose to do a multigenre writing project on dancing, which stemmed from a poem she created earlier in the year during a poetry unit (see Figure 3.1 for her poem).

Mary was very passionate about dancing and found poetry to be a terrific genre to write through. As she was looking through her writing portfolio, she was inspired by

FIGURE 3.1
Mary's Poem

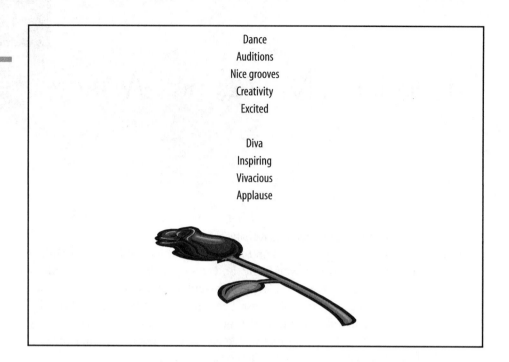

Dance
Auditions
Nice grooves
Creativity
Excited

Diva
Inspiring
Vivacious
Applause

her poem and the topic of dancing. Similarly, Becky, during a genre study of how-to books, created a business manual on how to sell a product. Figure 3.2 shows a sample from her book. As she was reviewing her writing portfolio, she came across this piece and decided advertising would make a very interesting topic.

We recommend that students select three possible topics for their first multigenre experience. During the preliminary investigation of each topic they may find there aren't enough resources to fully develop it or the topic is not exciting enough. By not narrowing in on one topic too quickly, they are less likely to be discouraged if this happens. The focus at this time is not on the genre inquiry, but rather on topics of potential interest. Most important, students are encouraged to find topics that matter and those they are passionate about.

Researching Possible Topics

Students, with the support of their peers and teacher, brainstorm topics from their searches that are deep enough to sustain their writing interests for several weeks or months. Additionally, their topic choice must support a rich variety of potential genre selections. As students think together, they frequently create hybrid choices—choices that are refined and revised through conversation. For instance, a student's original idea may be centered on a visit to Niagara Falls. After conversation, she might decide to expand this topic of one location to all of the current wonders of the world. Another child who also selected Niagara Falls may decide to target water and how it influences and affects the earth.

Typically multigenre writing includes a research focus (Allen 2001; Romano 2000) that requires a complex topic choice. For instance, children might select these various topics to support research investigations: endangered animals, the Battle of Yorktown,

FIGURE 3.2
Excerpt from Becky's How-to Book

7. Tell the customer your price and the prices of other companies compare them.

8. Don't make the consumer feel you're too friendly, you'll scare them.

9. Try to love your product.

10. Be honest. Don't lie and if you can't budge 1 person there are other people to persuade. These are your beginning guidelines to small and big success, have faith. Love what your product is, love what you do. Don't just be a salesperson but be a customer too. Love and live what you sell.

> Know and love the product
> Know the customer
> Have the knowledge.

wolves, the Dalai Lama, Helen Keller, the seven wonders of the world, and weather catastrophes. However, writing topics do not need to begin with a research focus; they may also develop from personal experiences and memoirs or personal interests. For example, students can create projects on topics such as dancing, family immigration to America, response to *Voices in the Park* (Browne 2001), cheerleading, and a celebration of family, just to name a few.

Topic choice is important for children to sustain a multigenre project. Taking time at this early point of the process will result in more engaged students throughout the project. It is typical for students to choose a topic, refine it, and abandon it as they shift to one that is more compelling.

Exploring and Investigating Multigenre Picture Books

As students are selecting their topics, teachers engage students in an exploration of multigenre picture books (multiple genres within one book). They highlight how a variety of genres add layers of meaning to a story (topic) and they ponder the strengths of particular genres in communicating ideas as well as limitations.

We share an example of this modeling from the classroom of Ali, a third-year teacher implementing multigenre writing. We detail how she guided her fifth-grade students through a multigenre picture book to sharpen their knowledge of genres and how they can complement each other within a single text.

Ali began one particular investigation by conducting a read-aloud of *The Jolly Postman* (Ahlberg and Ahlberg 2001). The book is a multigenre text that is filled with letters to fairy tale characters. The central character is a postman who delivers the mail to fairy tale characters. For instance, the witch from *Hansel and Gretel* receives a witch flyer advertising all the latest witch paraphernalia; the three bears receive an apology letter from Goldilocks; and Goldilocks sends an invitation to Baby Bear for her birthday party.

There are several genres present within the book: a friendly letter from Goldilocks; an advertisement sent to the witch; a postcard from Jack to the giant; a fairy tale picture book of Cinderella's story accompanied by a letter from a publishing company; a legal letter to the big bad wolf; and a birthday card and money for Goldilocks from Baby Bear and Mrs. Bunting. Each genre is enclosed in a separate envelope in the book, so it is easy for students to understand the differences in genre because they are not embedded within the text. They are distinct and offer students an explicit way to analyze each of them and to discover how they collectively enrich the text.

In the first discussion, Ali focused her student's attention on the picture book as a piece of art and literature. Her students engaged in a discussion of their thoughts and interpretations before analyzing the book to understand genre. She wanted them to understand the whole text and the humor that it contains.

After this initial appreciation of the text, Ali and her students completed an *impressions, connections, and wonderings chart* (Serafini 2001). On this chart they recorded their first impressions of the story, literary and personal connections, and wonderings they had about the text and the author. Figure 3.3 displays the final chart. In this discussion students made personal connections to the flyer received by the witch and literary connections to *The Stinky Cheeseman and Other Fairly Stupid Tales* by Jon Scieszka (1992). They also noted the unique language and identified some of the genres found within the book. Students also attended to their personal reactions; for example, one student commented, "It made me laugh."

The next day, Ali reread the book, and following the reading, she guided her students to identify the genres within the text. They made a list of all the genres that existed and discussed some preliminary ideas about each genre. For instance, Berto said, "The witch's advertisement has a voice like a used-car salesman." Students noticed that the letters were all from different points of view and told from a first- or third-person perspective. They decided that the third person was used when it was important for the piece or letter to reach a wide audience.

FIGURE 3.3
Impressions, Connections and Wonderings (ICW) Chart

T: *The Jolly Postman, or, Other People's Letters*
A: Janet and Allan Ahlberg
D: 4/26/06

Connections:
   T–S I get a catalog in the mail that was like the witch's catalog. Same kind of language and pictures.
   T–S We used a catalog, but we were on the other side trying to sell stuff for a fund-raiser.
   T–T Reminds me of Dr. Seuss, *Stinky Cheeseman,* fairy tales.
   T–S I wrote my own three little bears story in my own version.

Impressions:
   The book made me laugh, made me feel happy.
   The genres were letters, advertisements, postcard, books, and birthday card.
   Unique voice and style for each genre.
   Flashback in Goldilock's letter, illustrative foreshadowing.
   Setting was important.

Wonderings:
   How did the giant read?

After the whole-class discussion, the students were divided into small groups and each group received a copy of *The Jolly Postman*. The goal of the small groups was to discuss the individual genres within the book and how they impacted the book as a whole. To facilitate this discussion, Ali provided a discussion guide. The guide helped students think about particular characteristics of each individual genre within the book. The guide contained the following sections:

❖ Genre

❖ Language used in a particular genre

❖ Characteristics of a particular genre

❖ What is the perspective within the genre?

❖ Who is telling it?

❖ What can this genre do that others cannot?

Figure 3.4 is an example of a completed guide.

During this small-group investigation students discussed the book as a whole and selected one genre to focus on for the activity. In the example in Figure 3.4 the students examined the advertisement flyer the witch received from Hobgoblin Supplies Ltd. Students discussed the language and defined it as between formal and informal, much like commercial language, and identified the voice as being like a salesperson. They even identified an imaginary marketing department as the author of the piece.

As students discussed, Ali walked around the room, supporting their ideas and pushing them forward. It was not an easy assignment for the students. In the beginning they struggled to articulate what they knew about the advertisement genre. Through this discussion, students grasped the purpose of the genre as an isolated genre but then discovered the humor as they looked at the advertisement within the

---

Hobgoblin Supplies LTD

Genre
Ideas on voice: **sells persons voice**

Language used in genre: **it's in between casual and formal comersal language. Trying to sell something**

Characteristics of genre: **The catalogue has good displays each display has catch fraces.**

What is the perspective? (1st, 3rd, etc.): **The company is the perspective.**

Who is telling it? **The marketing department of Hobgoblin's supplies.**

What can this genre do that others cannot? **Show the producs it can make money off you, they benifet off of the producs.**

What can the genre add to the whole book? **It helps you understand witchs more. And there personality more.**

FIGURE 3.4
Completed Genre Discussion Guide

FIGURE 3.5
Integrated Genre Chart

	Catalog
Voice	excited, car salesman, happy, weaselly, tricky, exaggerated, joyful
Language	persuasive, descriptive, bribing, between formal and casual, adjectives help describe and persuade
Perspective	3rd person, supply company
Who's telling it?	marketing department
What can this genre do that others cannot?	sells stuff, goes to everyone (all witches), shows the products, benefit by making money, deceive people, advertise different products, not as personal
What does this genre add to the whole book?	every character in the book is getting mail, but all the mail is different types of communication

context of the whole book. As he became aware of the importance of audience, one student noted that if you were a witch, this would not be funny, rather, it would be informative.

After individual groups completed their guides, Ali reconvened the whole class to create an integrated chart (see Figure 3.5) to display all the ideas students had about all the genres in the book.

Through the discussions of each individual genre, students identified the variety of genres that occurred in the letters and shared responses to those particular genres. They discussed the importance, purpose, and effectiveness of the genres as well as how each one provided a unique perspective that other genres did not. They began to understand the nuanced differences in genres. They also moved beyond a discussion of genres and talked about the character traits of the fairy tale characters and each piece of mail they received.

Moving from this singular focus on individual genres, the students created a third chart, titled "What Does the Genre Add to the Whole Book?" To initiate the discussion, Ali asked each group to reread the book. Students needed to be drawn back to the text as a whole. Ali then asked students to contribute to the chart. Reactions to the synergistic relationship between text, illustrations, and genres were recorded.

Some ideas were

❖ It helps you understand the witch's personality more.

❖ It adds to the story because every fairy tale character is getting a different kind of mail.

❖ It made it funny and different.

❖ It makes the characters seem real because the letter is in an envelope.

❖ The letters make them believable like they are taking a break from their real life in the story.

These charts preserved students' thoughts for later reference. Students referred to the charts as they conducted similar investigations for their own topics, purposes, and genre choices.

Following this very scaffolded investigation of one text, the students moved to exploring multiple multigenre picture books. Each small group now received copies of one of the following: *Desert Seasons* (Devlin and Serafini 2003), *Dear Mrs. LaRue: Letters from Obedience School* (Teague 2002), *Crossing the Delaware* (Peacock 1998), *Snowflake Bentley* (Martin and Azarian 1998), or *The Secret Knowledge of Grown Ups* (Weisnewski 2001). Ali asked students to record the genres they found in each book and the responses they had to each genre. She used the same guide sheet as with the *Jolly Postman* activity (see Figure 3.4). She then asked them to read the book again and think about the text as a whole and how the individual genres influenced their overall reaction to the book. This independent investigation mirrored the one they had just completed with *The Jolly Postman.* She wanted students to think about the genres within the book, but she didn't want them to lose focus of the overall importance of the text when considered as a whole. After this three-day investigation, students gathered together and charted their findings and added to the integrated chart created during the *Jolly Postman* investigation (see Figure 3.5).

During this investigation, students analyzed the text their group was reading and recorded ideas on the guide sheet. Ali asked them to consider the effectiveness of one genre and how each piece within a text added to the richness of the text as a whole. She wanted them to discover the layering effect each genre had on the overall meaning of the book. At the end of this investigation, Ali asked her students to record ideas they had gathered for their own writing pieces in their writer's notebooks. Ali wanted students to connect what they were doing during these investigations to their own writing purposes. Each day during writing time, Ali conferred with students and asked them to share what they had recorded in their notebooks and how the investigation of multigenre texts helped them envision their own writing projects.

She learned that students recognized that one genre did not tell the whole story. For example, Keisha read *Crossing the Delaware* by Louise Peacock (1998). She wrote in her notebook that the letters from the soldier and his girlfriend offered a personal perspective to the Revolutionary War and the events leading to the crossing of the Delaware, yet they did not offer the historical facts like the narration and the journal entries from the generals did. Each of the three genres provided different information and perspectives on that time in history. The investigations of multigenre picture books allowed Ali to have a discussion with her students about the possibilities of their own multigenre projects and how each genre could provide a different yet crucial window into their chosen topics.

Investigating Multiple Texts Centered on a Single Topic

Once students are comfortable with identifying and discussing genres from a single text, it is time for them to investigate multiple texts representing various genres. Through an exploration of multiple texts, they learn how texts, in addition to a single book, represent multiple genres and how understanding one text adds to the understanding of another. The focus is on the power of genre and how each genre provides a new and different understanding of a particular topic.

We use the following example with the Grand Canyon as a central topic as a model for these more complex investigations. To begin this exploration, Suzette brought in many texts of various genres on this topic. She formed investigative groups to look at each text and to analyze its genre and what kind of information, perspective, and purpose it brought to the topic.

Each group analyzed their individual reactions to each type of genre. Suzette added a few questions to the *Jolly Postman* sheet and had students use it to guide their discussions. The additional questions were

❖ How did the text/genre help you to understand the topic?

❖ What are the limitations of this topic or genre?

❖ How is the information presented?

❖ Are there multiple genres within any of the texts?

The investigation was conducted in much the same manner as the multigenre picture book investigation. Students created small-group charts to identify the genre, describe the characteristics of that particular genre, and describe how that genre added to knowledge of the Grand Canyon. Students made a chart for each of the genres to record descriptions of genres and possible purposes for each. See Appendix A for a text set list about the Grand Canyon.

These discussions provided an avenue for children to explore their responses to a variety of genres on a single topic. After the investigative small groups shared information about their genre, they discovered how their particular genre provided one perspective on the topic while another group's offered a different perspective. These varied views and genres contributed to a new more expansive understanding of the Grand Canyon. This type of investigation goes further than an investigation of a single genre or multiple genres within a single book in that it explores the dimensions reached by each particular genre and how they influence the understanding of a topic through a whole text set.

Exploring Multigenre Projects

As students conclude an investigation of multiple genres as a whole class, it is time to transition into perusing student-created multigenre projects. Teachers like Ali and Suzette, who have engaged students in multigenre writing over previous years, can share past student projects as models for current students. Students can explore the topics students have investigated and how they have used multiple genres to share facets of their projects. Finally, they can discover how each of these pieces contributes to the whole project and how each piece enhances or extends the knowledge from a previous one.

There are also numerous websites that can aid in this investigation as well. The National Council of Teachers of English (www.ncte.org) has many examples and resources for those interested in multigenre writing. Similarly, the International

Reading Association and the National Council of Teachers of English, through its Read-Write-Think project (www.ReadWriteThink.org) have many lesson plans for launching and discussing multigenre text. These resources can be used as teachers build a collection of student projects. Through these websites and others like them, teachers can find models to support them and their students as they first gain knowledge of multigenre writing. We share numerous examples in Chapter 5 where we outline many approaches to multigenre writing.

Narrowing in on a Topic

After students have had opportunities to mine their writing notebooks and have participated in the lessons described thus far, it is time for them to each settle on a topic of personal interest. When the exploration into multiple genres is coming to a close, students are expected to finalize their topics. Students who struggle with this decision might go online to see whether their topic is rich enough for a multigenre project. They can also use people resources like their family or other students to see what others believe about potential information on their topic.

Once topics are selected, create a class list so that all students are aware of the topics of their peers. With this knowledge, they are better able to support one another throughout this project. Students may choose to work independently or in small groups as they gather information about their topics, and group organization can be facilitated by topic choice. Once students have begun this investigative work and they are convinced their topic is substantial, they move to the next phase of their project—a proposal.

The Proposal

The proposal is a demonstration of students' preliminary ideas about their topic and the genres they have selected. Students present their beginning thoughts and propose for themselves and the teacher how they want their overall project to look. Figure 3.6 is an incomplete proposal form to get you started. The form includes space for only one genre. You will need to add space for as many genres as you'll be requiring for the multigenre writing project. Figure 3.7 displays Ty's completed proposal for his first genre.

Reason for Choosing the Topic

The proposal asks students to reflect on why they chose their topic. This metacognitive thinking helps students clarify the importance of their topic. As students identify their personal importance, they then may begin to decide on ways to communicate their ideas for this topic and how the complete multigenre project will look as each genre contributes a different lens on the topic. As students justify their reasons it helps them hone in on what topics will sustain five or six writing projects and keeps students from frivolously choosing a topic at the last minute.

FIGURE 3.6
Incomplete Proposal

Multigenre Writing Proposal

Name: _____   Topic: _____

Reasons for choosing this topic:

_____
_____
_____
_____
_____
_____

1st Genre: _____

Definition of this genre:

_____
_____
_____
_____
_____
_____
_____

Perspective (Who is writing?):

_____
_____

Audience (Who is reading?):

_____
_____

Purpose for writing:

_____
_____
_____
_____

Genre and Definition

Once the topic has been identified, students then need to name their chosen genres and provide a preliminary definition for each. We say preliminary because as students delve into the writing and research, this definition will sharpen with exposure to more and more examples of the genre. The definitions will certainly be stronger for those genres children have been exposed to in school or routinely at home and less definitive for different or unfamiliar genres. A definition might be based on characteristics or style of writing. How children define their genres will be scaffolded from the single-genre explorations. How a teacher demonstrates defining genre will impact how students define genre independently. Referring to Figure 3.7, it is evident that Ty was familiar with his topic, the NBA, yet he wanted to discover the topic through new genres.

In other pages of his proposal Ty identified a variety of genres to explore, including a newspaper article, a poster, a calendar, and a journal entry, and had a

FIGURE 3.7
Ty's Completed Proposal

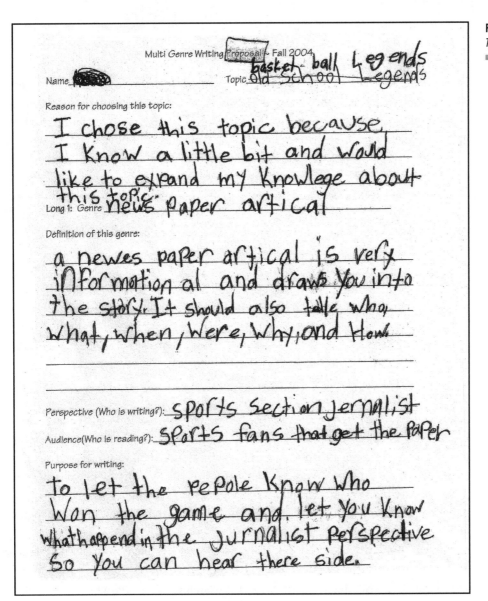

Multi Genre Writing Proposal - Fall 2004

Name_____ Topic: Old School Legends
basket-ball Legends

Reason for choosing this topic:

I chose this topic because
I know a little bit and would
like to expand my knowlege about
this topic.

Long 1: Genre news paper artical

Definition of this genre:

a newes paper artical is very
informational and draws you into
the story. It should also tell who,
what, when, were, why, and How

Perspective (Who is writing?): sports section jernalist

Audience(Who is reading?): sports fans that get the paper

Purpose for writing:

to let the repole know who
won the game and let you know
whathappend in the jurnalist perspective
So you can hear there side.

good grasp of their communicative purposes. Ty defined his newspaper genre as "very informational and draws you into the story. It should also tell who, what, when, where, why, and how." In this definition of genre, Ty displayed his knowledge of the genre as he stated that a newspaper article should inform yet it should also be in a style of writing that will capture the reader's attention. He also attended to the well-known five Ws.

Perspective

Students are asked to identify the perspective of each genre. The proposal asks students to identify who is writing the piece. What is interesting about a multigenre writing project is that children can write from first or third person and from the perspective of any person who might authentically write a piece in regard to that topic. For example, Anna wanted to address the impact of graffiti in her neighborhood, so she chose to write from a wall's perspective; in two of her pieces she personified a wall and wrote as if it had feelings. In another multigenre writing project, Lisa chose the *Titanic* as her topic; in two of her pieces she wrote journal entries, one from a person who survived and another from a passenger's last minutes on the *Titanic*.

Students choose which perspective will be the most effective. As students begin to investigate their intended genres, they make note of the point of view each genre typically takes. For instance, Ty noted that sport columns are typically written from a sports journalist's perspective and from the third-person point of view.

Audience

As students make decisions about the perspective of their pieces they simultaneously decide on the audience for their various genres. Writers at times choose the audience first, as with Anna—she knew she wanted to target gang members in her community for one of her pieces. Her next decision was to decide which perspective and genre would do that most effectively. Audience plays a pivotal role in the construction of writing pieces. The audience drives the choice of genre, the language, the structure, the features, and most certainly the voice of the piece. This is not a new concept in the teaching of writing, yet making it explicit in the proposal ensures that children consider the audience simultaneously as they construct their multigenre writing project.

Purpose for Writing

As a student shares his topic, the purpose behind his choice of topic will begin to outline his genre choices. For example, Anna's topic of walls and graffiti was important to her as it affected her friends and family. During discussion of this topic with her classmates, the topic morphed and became larger as she thought about walls all over the world and their symbolic importance. When she talked about this larger purpose of her paper, she considered genre possibilities and how they would contribute to her paper individually and collectively.

In order to create the proposal, students use the language from the investigation on genres to articulate what each genre piece will bring to their overall topic. This kind of prewriting and thinking is invaluable. It moves children beyond writing for just classmates and teachers, as students must attend to their intended audience as they write from a variety of perspectives for a variety of purposes. It also requires them to have an understanding of the purposes of various genres and requires them to make decisions about the communicative power of each genre. It moves away from assigning genre and asks students to choose genres for various purposes and effects.

Moreover, this kind of writing project bridges the gap of home and school literacies as students choose to write through genres typically found in school such as narratives, poetry, letters, journals, and reports and those found outside of school such as commercials, newspaper advertisements, applications, memos, blogs, websites, postcards, and obituaries. Students choose genres that are culturally relevant as they match topic and genre for particular communicative purposes.

Genre Possibilities

As students work on their proposal, the teacher and students continue to add to a list of brainstormed genres. The list began at the beginning of the multigenre investigation and is continued throughout the project. Once the list is somewhat complete, the teacher and students can decide which genres are expected in school or out of school. They might also explore those from state standards and discover which ones fit this list. They will quickly discover how much more they know about genres than is typically expected in state standards.

To expand on this list of genres and students' general awareness of genres, students can explore the following website: www.sheboyganfalls.k12.wi.us/cyberenglish9/ multi_genre/genre_types.htm#advice%20columns. This site lists genres and provides descriptions of each. After perusing the site, the classroom can expand its list. This expansion allows students to review their genre choices and to revise by including new genres. For example, Brittany chose marine biology as a topic and she envisioned herself as a marine biologist someday, but she was not familiar with résumés. She was interested in pursuing this genre so her teacher brought several examples of résumés to school and together they discussed the purpose and language within this particular genre. The result was that she included this genre in her project (see Figure 3.8).

Bringing Unity to the Project

Once students complete the proposal and create an expansive list of genres, it is time to consider the project as a unified whole. Moving from the discussion on individual genres, students now pursue a focus for their projects as a literary unit. Students, with their teacher's guidance, return to previous charts to remember the importance of how each genre contributed uniquely to the whole in their investigations of various genres and multigenre picture books.

Structure of the Multigenre Project

Students are introduced to the overall layout of the project while they are working on their proposals. Each part of the project can be constructed at various times, and lengthier explicit lessons for each are detailed in the next chapter. The multigenre project includes

- ❖ a cover;
- ❖ an introduction;
- ❖ an outline or table of contents;
- ❖ defenses for each piece;
- ❖ three to six writing pieces; and
- ❖ visual designs or graphic elements.

The following sections detail some of the elements and illuminate them with various examples.

FIGURE 3.8
Brittany's Resume

BRITTANY

OBJECTIVE

To obtain employment in an environment where I can challenge my experience and standards as a professional marine biologist.

EXPERIENCE

2020–2022   Marine World   San Diego, CA
National Marine Doctor/Trainer
- Increased animal health from 23% to 69%.
- Made environment more natural.
- Increased crowd and sales for passes to get in.

2022–2024   Sea World   Jacksonville Beach, FL
Private Sector Marine Health/Trainer/Instructor
- Increased sales of park tickets.
- Managed medication for injection.
- Improved natural environment to increase life span.

2024–2025   Shedd Aquarium   Chicago, IL
Head of Health and Trainer to Animals
- Increased health from 19% to 86%.
- Trained for private shows.
- Helped give birth to 8 marine animals.

EDUCATION

2013–2020   Brooks Institute of Santa Barbara
- Marine and Computer Science.
- Health for animals.
- Moleculer Biology.

INTERESTS

My interests are manager of research and to experience old and new things.

FAX (888) 694-3872 · E-MAIL ME AT WWW.PROMARINE.COM
MARINE CENTER · LIHUE, KAUAII · WORLDWIDE · PHONE (888) 684-8862

Introduction

Students need to consider how this project shares a unified focus even though it consists of a variety of genres put together under a single cover. Each piece must work together to share information about the topic or have some connecting thread throughout to pull the piece together. In an effort to do this, students are expected to write an introduction to their multigenre project.

The introduction is in a narrative form, speaking directly to the reader. This piece and the defense are the only two places where students typically speak from their own perspective. In this section they explain the various perspectives and points of view they will be writing from. The introduction identifies the purposes and interests in the topic and shares with the reader why the student made the choices that were important to the project's creation.

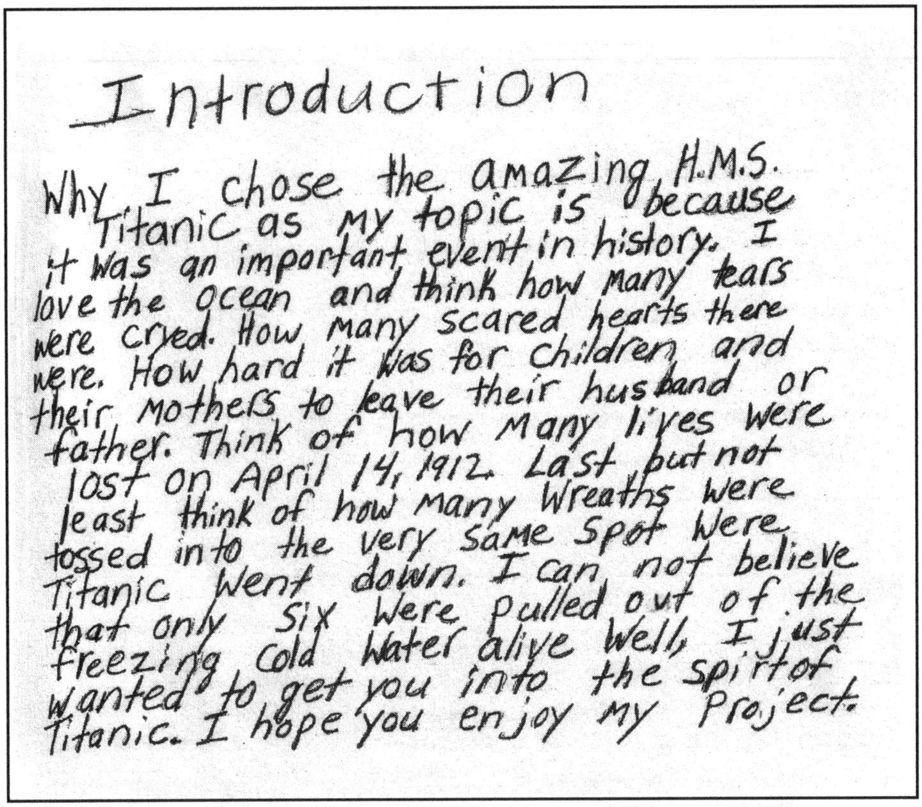

FIGURE 3.9
Lisa's Introduction About the
Titanic *Project*

> ## Introduction
>
> Why I chose the amazing, H.M.S. Titanic as my topic is because it was an important event in history. I love the ocean and think how many tears were cried. How many scared hearts there were. How hard it was for children and their mothers to leave their husband or father. Think of how many lives were lost on April 14, 1912. Last but not least think of how many wreaths were tossed into the very same spot were Titanic went down. I can not believe that only six were pulled out of the freezing cold water alive. Well, I just wanted to get you into the spirit of Titanic. I hope you enjoy my project.

In the introduction a student explains the relationship between each piece and shares the purposes for each and how a reader might go about enjoying and reading the project. In Figure 3.9, Lisa shares the spirit of her writing. She shares the history of the *Titanic* and why it is so important to her.

In contrast, Katie explains why each of her pieces exists in her introduction. She focuses on each piece rather than on the history of her project (see Figure 3.10). The introduction helps the reader understand the writer's choices and how each piece is connected to the topic.

The Defense

A critical piece to the multigenre project is the defense. A defense is attached to each piece and explains why the writing piece should exist. The defense has particular requirements. Students must explain

❖ who the audience is;

❖ why the piece exists;

❖ characteristics of the genre; and

❖ the perspective and purpose of the genre.

As with the introduction, students have essential questions they must answer in a defense, but they are invited to turn it into a narrative form again, speaking directly to the reader. Some students look at the defense as a way to tell the reader how to read a piece, while other students give voice and purpose to the defense, truly creating another genre and writing piece altogether. For example, Anna used

FIGURE 3.10
Katie's Introduction

INTRODUCTION

I chose to do this book about me because I love to write and learn about myself.

Letter to Friend—I wrote this letter to Amber because it is important that she know what I think of her.

Self Portrait—I drew this picture of me because I want people to know my perspective of what I think I look like.

Interview—I wrote this interview because I want people to know a little more about me. I am using receiving an award as an example.

Autobiography—I wrote this autobiography because I want it so that people can learn a little about me and about my family and friends.

FIGURE 3.11
Anna's Defense of a Bumper Sticker

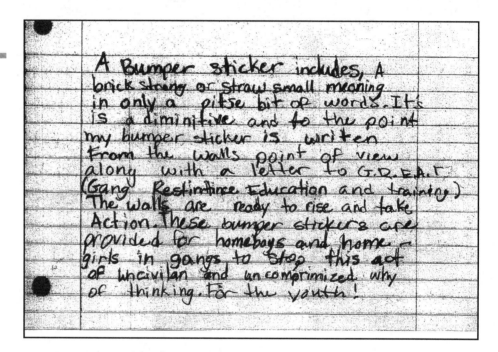

her defense to shape her writing. In an interview she described the defense in this manner:

> The defense, it's like you're trying to write from the perspective of, well, for my project the perspective of the wall, and then you're also writing from the perspective of yourself. So you have to write from two voices into a defense so I think that, yeah, my projects they grew more from my defenses cuz since I switch off from my defenses to my project and it gave me more of an idea of perspective into my writing.

See Anna's defense of her bumper sticker in Figure 3.11.

Some students write the defense once the writing piece has been completed like Ty's defense of his fictitious interview with Magic Johnson (see Figure 3.12). He explained his defense in this manner:

FIGURE 3.12
Ty's Defense of an Interview

I wrote an interview with Magic Johnson so you can hear his perspective of what happened when Julius Irving did his hang time move. My audience is anyone who reads the sports section. Some special characters of an interview are only the questions are planned the answers can be anything. This piece exists so you can hear the real side of a professional who was really there.

If you read the defense first it might make my piece sound a little different cuz you know exactly why I wrote it and who I was thinking about for my perspective but if you read it afterwards it might be a whole different kind of piece. Like if I started out with a book and I did not look at the back I would not really know what the story was about at first so if you start out mine I think the story could really be different . . . so I think it just really changed your view of the writing pieces.

Once he was done he reviewed his piece and defended why the piece should exist and the qualities found in an interview. Anna, on the other hand, used her defense to guide her writing as she went through numerous drafts of her defense of a bumper sticker. Anna used this defense to hone in on her understanding of what a bumper sticker is and its communicative purposes. Often, students like to take a break from the writing of their genre pieces, either because they are stuck or because they just want a change, so they may begin writing their defense or turn to another piece of writing.

Visual Elements

Artistic expression is an important element in the multigenre writing project. The versatility of this project lends itself to all kinds of learners and writers. Students who are more artistically inclined have a great outlet for communicating their ideas through some sort of visual design. Multimodal representation connects with the fast-paced world of Internet reading and advertisements. In this project students are required to illustrate their writing pieces or create a visual design that can stand as its own genre.

Many times students illustrate their covers or illustrate their writing pieces. Others have chosen PowerPoint, posters, banners, commercials, flyers, brochures, maps, battle plans, architecture plans, diagrams of animals, or models to represent their learning of a particular topic. Multigenre writing affords writers the opportunity to experiment with many modes of representation. (See Figures 3.13 and 3.14 for examples of students' visual elements.)

The proposal and introductory phase typically lasts two to three weeks. It is a necessary time to help students envision the possibilities of their writing pieces and as many authors have explained (Fletcher 2001; Nia 1999; Wood Ray 2001), the prewriting and immersion stages of the project help students gather a plethora of information so that once they begin writing, it is relatively easy and clear for them.

During the first half of the year, time is spent discovering and investigating single genres. Throughout that investigation students learn how to go about examining genres and they now are able to do it independently or in small genre groups. Once students have the proposal, a list of genres to choose from, and an understanding of the project as a whole, they are prepared to construct their multigenre writing pieces as they investigate familiar and unfamiliar genres for their own writing purposes.

FIGURE 3.13
A Student's Visual Element

References

Ahlberg, J., and A. Ahlberg. 2001. *The Jolly Postman, or, Other People's Letters.* New York: Little, Brown.

Allen, C. A. 2001. *The Multigenre Research Paper: Voice, Passion and Discovery in Grades 4–6.* Portsmouth, NH: Heinemann.

Browne, A. 2001. *Voices in the Park.* New York: DK.

Devlin, R., and F. Serafini. 2003. *Desert Seasons.* Las Vegas: Stephens.

Fletcher, R. 2001. *The Writing Workshop: The Essential Guide.* Portsmouth, NH: Heinemann.

Martin, J., and M. Azarian. 1998. *Snowflake Bentley.* Boston: Houghton Mifflin.

Nia, I. 1999. "Units of Study in the Writing Workshop." *Primary Voices K–6* 8 (1), 3–12.

Peacock, L. 1998. *Crossing the Delaware.* New York: Simon and Schuster.

FIGURE 3.14
Another Student's Visual Element

Romano, T. 2000. *Blending Genre, Altering Style: Writing Multigenre Papers.* Portsmouth, NH: Boynton/Cook.

Scieszka, J. 1992. *The Stinky Cheeseman and Other Fairly Stupid Tales.* New York: Viking.

Serafini, F. 2001. *The Reading Workshop: Creating Space for Readers.* Portsmouth, NH: Heinemann.

Teague, M. 2002. *Dear Mrs. LaRue: Letters from Obedience School.* New York: Scholastic.

Weisnewski, D. 2001. *The Secret Knowledge of Grown Ups.* New York: HarperTrophy.

Wood Ray, K. 2001. *The Writing Workshop: Working through the Hard Parts (And They're All Hard Parts).* Urbana, IL: NCTE.

CHAPTER 4

Teaching and Managing Multigenre Writing

ANNA: We brainstormed some ideas of what you could write for a multigenre project. I did it last year and we added more that other kids thought of and we started growing that list.

TEACHER: So students added genres to the list. So why did you decide to write a graffiti wall? To create one?

ANNA: Because normally kids would do that to walls, and then I thought it would be fun for a wall talking and explaining to the kids why they shouldn't do it and that the wall has feelings and stuff like that.

TEACHER: Can you explain why you decided on all of your genres, and do you think they were good choices?

ANNA: I think they were a good choice but I think I could have done more if I had more time. I could have put in other genres and made them better.

TEACHER: Why did you choose the ones that you did?

ANNA: I think because they fit the best. They sounded like fun. I could go deeper into it. Like a PowerPoint people would normally do, like make it all fun with sound effects and everything like that, but I really focused on what the wall was trying to say and I focused more on the content instead of the animations.

In this conversation, which occurred at the end of a multigenre project, Anna was reflecting on her project with her teacher. Clearly Anna was quite thoughtful as she reflected on her project and her choices. Her teacher was inquisitive about her choices and the process of creating the multigenre project. This brief conversation shared the results of the process of multigenre writing. We know that teachers are wondering about the steps that were put into place to achieve such thoughtful, reflective dialogue about the project. This chapter provides all of the details for teacher and student success.

In this chapter we outline ways to choreograph the writing workshop to support children's independence and understanding of the multigenre writing project. We describe a series of whole- and small-group instruction and discussion as well as peer conferencing and teacher-student conferences. Whole-class instruction occurs more frequently at the beginning of the draft stage, as these lessons focus on supporting children's attempts at organizing, researching, and writing and occur as needed in response to writers' needs. The small-group instruction focuses on genre knowledge and negotiation of characteristics for genres. In these groups teacher and students read critically and examine characteristics across genres, attending to similarities, traits, and patterns unique to specific genres. Individual conferences help the writer stay on track and work on voice and perspective of the piece, and they are concerned with the individual writer.

As students are writing from a variety of perspectives on a variety of topics, it is important for them to utilize the predictability of the writing workshop and write independently while the teacher works with various small groups and individual writers. Many whole-class lessons introduce a topic, process, or idea that will be carried out or maintained throughout individual and small-group formats and investigations.

Whole-Class Lessons

Helping Children Become Independent for Writing Time

In order to scaffold children's independence for a multigenre writing project, a series of whole-class lessons on a variety of organizing topics is very useful. Typically in the

FIGURE 4.1
An Example of a Class Time Line

Name _____   Topic _____

Requirements and Due Dates for Multigenre Writing Project

Required Elements	Due
____ Proposal Form	_____
____ Rough Drafts 1 & 2	_____
____ Rough Drafts 3 & 4	_____
____ Defenses 1 & 2	_____
____ Defenses 3 & 4	_____
____ Final Project	_____
____ Cover	_____
____ About the Author or Introduction	_____
____ Genre 1	_____
____ Genre 2	_____
____ Genre 3	_____
____ Genre 4	_____
____ 4 Defenses (one for each piece)	_____
CELEBRATION	_____

writing workshop the whole-class lessons are reserved for information all students can use. During a multigenre writing project, the purpose remains the same. As it is a complex writing project, it is important to begin with ways that students can manage their writing time and manage all of their writing projects. Through this organization students are free to pursue research and writing endeavors without the direct help of the teacher each time they need to make a decision.

Making a Time Line

In Ali's classroom, she and her students negotiated a time line for the multigenre writing project. Figure 4.1 is an example of her class time line. The students and teacher together discussed how much time they needed to complete each piece and its defense as well as negotiated time for revision and editing. Then ultimately they chose a date for publication. A time line gives writers power over their writing time, it is not imposed on them and they learn about the real world of deadlines and management of time. Students need approximately six to eight weeks for completion. Of course this will vary with the grade level and the number of pieces that a teacher expects students to complete. In this example, students were expected to complete four pieces with defenses. In the primary grades students might be expected to complete only two or three.

How to Manage and Organize the Writing Pieces

One of the struggles with multigenre writing is keeping all the writing organized. As pointed out earlier, keeping drafts in desks is never a good idea. In Suzette's and Ali's classrooms, they used a variety of strategies to help students stay organized, which were addressed in whole-class minilessons. Ali and Suzette demonstrated how to use a writer's notebook for ideas, how to transfer an idea to the draft book, and then how to begin a more permanent draft for publication. In theses lessons, Suzette and Ali both negotiated with students the best way to organize and store their writing.

First students use a spiral-bound notebook for their writer's notebook, where pages are attached and safe. As students transition into the draft phase, they use another spiral notebook called their draft book. Third, as students are ready to begin publishing, they put loose papers in a portfolio box that is centrally located in the classroom. Also, each student has a file for her multigenre writing either on a file server or on the computer itself, as much of the publishing for these projects is completed on the computer.

Time to organize is also an important consideration. When writing time is completed, it is essential that students have enough time to save their work properly on the computer or file server and it is important for students to be able to easily access their portfolios to place their writing in. If this transition time is rushed, students cram all their work into strange places, and it might never be seen again. This aspect is certainly something that is practiced all year long so that during a multigenre writing project students are accustomed to the procedures and will not fear losing their pieces. During a multigenre writing project, students can have up to thirteen or fourteen writing pieces in progress, so organization is of the utmost concern. In this section we provide only one example for organization; many options are available, but the important thing is to choose a system and implement it early in the year. Teachers may need to maintain procedures with minilessons throughout the year as the need arises.

Writing Workshop Options

Once procedures for saving and organizing work are firmly into place, it is helpful for children to have writing workshop options. Wood Ray (2001) emphasizes the importance of options for writers to choose from to begin writing in their writer's notebook. She shares many ways for children to engage in the writing process so that they are not waiting for assistance from the teacher and thus losing valuable writing time. In her suggestions she even makes a case for "staring off into space" (66), since thinking about a writing topic is a valuable writing strategy as well.

During the multigenre writing project, students have thought a great deal about their writing project as they completed the proposal, and so they are ready to begin writing drafts. They may work on any of the pieces at any time, and this provides choice and freedom for writing. As children write they typically work on one piece for a little while and then begin to draft their defense. As Anna described earlier, her defense helped her construct her writing piece:

> I think that my projects grew more from my defenses because since I switch off from my defenses to my project it gave me more of an idea of perspective into my writing.

This flexibility certainly helps to manage computer time; if the computers are being used for an extended period of time, then students have many other options to choose from and therefore are not stuck for the rest of writing time. Both Ali and Suzette created charts to list the options for writing time so students could refer to them at any time (see Figure 4.2).

This chart was created during a whole-class lesson so students could decide which options were appropriate and could discuss as a class ways of becoming independent when the teacher was working with small groups or individual writers. This chart was an evolving document—students and the teacher added to it as new options became available.

Weekly Goals

We have found multigenre weekly goal sheets to be a tremendous help to both the student and the teacher. Figure 4.3 is an example of a multigenre goal sheet for teachers to use.

To begin, the teacher describes the goal sheet to the whole class and on the overhead completes one for all the students to see and discuss. Students then fill out their

FIGURE 4.2
Multigenre Writing Workshop Options

1. Read and research your topic.
   a. Resources: computer, books, people, mentor text
2. Begin draft of any of the pieces.
3. Work on introduction.
4. Write defenses for pieces.
5. Illustrate any writing piece or cover to your multigenre project.
6. Peer conference with a classmate.
7. Help another student with research.
8. Pair read with a student writing in the same genre.
9. Read, discuss, and analyze any books within the same genre.

FIGURE 4.3
Multigenre Goal Sheet

Multigenre Weekly Goal Sheet

Goals for the week:

What I need to do today:	What worked—what was a struggle:
Monday	
Tuesday	
Wednesday	
Thursday	
Friday	
Reflection on last week's goal:	

first multigenre goal sheet together, with the support of the class and teacher, as they are able to ask questions and discuss the process. After the first whole-class demonstration, goals are then maintained and created through small-group goal-setting meetings.

Each student receives a goal sheet each week and the teacher conducts weekly meetings to help create, work toward, and reflect on her weekly writing goals. These meetings and sheets help children to be cognizant of their work and struggles they may be encountering. It also acts as an assessment tool for the teacher to document work completed each week, especially between deadlines. It provides another avenue for the teacher to see and discuss children's writing.

One way of managing these meetings is to group students by alphabetical order and meet with five or six students each day. Assign each group a day or some rotating schedule and meet with a small group at the beginning of the writing workshop for about ten minutes. We have found this to be an easy way to meet with all students and still have time to manage the writing workshop.

In these meetings students bring the previous week's goal sheets and any completed work for the week. To begin the conversation the teacher will say, "How did your week go?" Students will refer to the previous week's goal sheets and discuss their successes and any roadblocks to meeting their goals. This kind of discussion puts the children in control of setting and meeting goals and allows the teacher to scaffold goal setting to make sure the goals are reasonable for each child. Students and teacher offer advice and celebrate successes. It is also a way for children to share any resources they may have found during their week of writing that might be of value to other students.

These meetings are a great accountability tool as well as instructional tool. The students expect the meeting and know they are going to be held accountable for their work for the week. The teacher then files their goal sheets into a three-ring binder for later reference and safekeeping. The goal sheet creates a daily checklist for children and helps them to remain on task during independent time. The goal-setting meeting also allows children to celebrate all they have accomplished during the week.

Then students receive a new sheet and begin to set goals for the coming week. Once they write them down they discuss the goals they have set and organize their goal sheet to help them with daily tasks as well as their overall weekly goals. See Figure 4.4 for Cassie's second grade completed weekly goal sheet.

Students are expected to use this sheet on a daily basis to help them focus on what they need to do in a busy writing workshop environment.

Peer Conferences

Peer conferencing for multigenre writing projects can take many forms. Students can get together to discuss a particular genre and the characteristics found within their classroom examples, they can help with a particular genre piece, help with the creation and effectiveness of their defenses, or help each other with the unity of their project.

Peer conferencing with multigenre writing moves beyond traditional single-piece conferencing and asks different kinds of questions. See Figure 4.5 for an example of this peer conference form.

This form asks the *editor* to consider the unity the piece has with the project theme as a whole and to consider the audience, perspective, and authenticity of the piece as well as make suggestions to the writer for making the piece stronger. These kinds of questions move the pair beyond "Does the writing make sense?" and ask them to consider the purpose of their writing.

In order to have successful productive peer conferences, much time must be taken to model the kinds of conversations and responses the teacher and students expect from each other. The teacher can model this kind of conference with his own writing, with another student, or with a fellow teacher. Another teacher can come into the

FIGURE 4.4
Cassie's Goal Sheet

Multigenre Weekly Goal Sheet

Goals for the week:

Read Ruby.B Book
get Leter done

What I need to do today: | What worked-What was a struggle

Monday
\ Read Story | Reading dering noise. Withting time

Tuesday
✓ Read Story | Whent in hall finished Book

Wednesday
✓ Write letter
✓ | Hard to deside Who was Writeing it

Thursday
✓ Write Letter
✓ Watched move on RubyB | Sally worte the Letter

Friday
Letter | I wanted to write because i knew What to Say

Reflection on last week's goals:

Once I Knew who was Writing it was Easier

---

classroom or the conference can be videotaped for future reference or for use in other classrooms. However it is done, it is important for the teacher to model how to get beyond "I like your writing piece."

Some of the most influential modeling already occurred during the single-genre analysis of published text. During whole-class and small-group literature discussions, students were taught how to analyze the text for perspective, authenticity, and the purpose the genre served. Students were shown that these conversations could also occur during a peer writing conference. Students cannot be expected to be successful if this is the first time they are asked to think deeply about a text. These conversations are scaffolded over time.

A fishbowl strategy (Serafini 2006) that is typically used to enhance literary discussions can be utilized for peer conference discussions as well. To adapt a fishbowl for peer conferencing, a teacher selects two or three students who have exhibited sufficient strategies for peer conferencing and places them in the middle with one

FIGURE 4.5
Peer Conference Form

Peer Conference Form

Date:

Author's Name:

Editor's Name:

Title of Piece:

_____ I understand why this piece exists.

_____ I know who the audience is.

_____ I know whose perspective it is written from.

Ideas on how the piece fits with the topic and the whole project:

I really like these things about your piece:

These are some ideas that I think would make your piece stronger:

student's multigenre writing, while the rest of the class sits in a circle around them. The students in the center conduct a peer conference and the students on the outside act as researchers, observing and taking notes on the process and dialogue used in the conference. At the conclusion of the peer conference, the students discuss the effectiveness of the conference and make note of any ways in which they could enhance the conference. Other students are then welcomed into the middle and the modeling continues. Obviously this is a strategy to be utilized in the beginning of the year, but it needs to be modeled again for the specific needs of multigenre writing.

Peer conferencing during a multigenre writing unit can be very helpful to move children forward with their writing. Once small-group investigations have begun on various genres, students seek out those members writing within similar genres for peer conferencing and other times they choose someone they feel safe to share their writing with, like a friend. However they choose their partners, the dialogue that has occurred all year long about text and various genres and the scaffolding of peer conference formats support them in their endeavors to discuss their own writing pieces.

Use of Technology for Research

Just because students have created a proposal does not mean that they have completed their research; on the contrary, the proposal represents a very preliminary understanding of their topic and genres. Students continue to research not only their topic but also their genres. During whole-class lessons it becomes important for the teacher to demonstrate using technology as a research tool. In the intermediate grades students are certainly familiar with the Internet and electronic resources but need help in locating and evaluating sources found on CD-ROMs and the Internet.

The use of think-alouds can be a powerful way to show students how to navigate and make meaning of electronic sources. A think-aloud can be achieved by projecting various websites for children to see. In this manner it is easy to locate more obscure examples of genres like death certificates, marriage certificates, lists, blog entries, emails, brochures, resumes, lesson plans, and so on. During a think-aloud a teacher can demonstrate to students the importance of identifying the source of the piece, the authenticity, the purpose for writing it, the effectiveness of the piece, and how the visual graphics enhance or persuade the reader in some particular way. See Figure 4.6 for a partial transcript of Suzette's think-aloud for the Grand Canyon Geology website www.edu-source.com/GCpages/CVOpage1.html.

In her think-aloud she discussed her Google search and how she chose the particular site. She then continued to think aloud as she navigated through the website, identifying particular characteristics and how she was constructing meaning. In this think-aloud she demonstrated the understanding of the online expository text while attending to the expository elements of question and answer. She highlighted the simultaneity of the text and images and how they together affected her understanding and response to the genre. She understood that it was equally important to attend to both images and text just as she does in her reading of picture books with students.

In another series of think-alouds, Suzette demonstrated how to use the Internet to research a topic. She navigated through a series of websites on various topics that students had chosen. These think-alouds allowed the students to see how they could find the information they needed without getting bogged down by tedious and/or misleading information.

After the think-alouds are completed it is necessary to ask students to comment on the strategies that you highlighted and to think about which strategies will prove useful for them in their search for information and investigation of genres. It is also important to help students understand the difference between electronic sources and those that are typically found on paper but have been transferred onto the Internet, like certificates.

I see that the title is Grand Canyon Geology. The subheading is Rim to River: The Geological Layers of the Grand Canyon. The creator of this web page wants us to attend to the colors and the slice of the Grand Canyon that is found as soon as we open this site. The rest of the information we find will be about the layers of the Grand Canyon.

FIGURE 4.6
Suzette's Think-Aloud

Write-Aloud: Introduction and Defenses

In addition to thinking aloud, writing aloud can be useful. A write-aloud is the same as a think-aloud but you think aloud as you write in front of the students either on an overhead projector or by typing on the computer and projecting it onto a screen. At an NCTE conference Donald Graves (2003) made the case for writing in front of students as he demonstrated his thought process about how to initiate writing on a childhood memory. He believes teachers need to demonstrate the writing and thought process in the act of writing, where children need the most support. Some components of the multigenre writing project are new to students and this modeling provides the necessary support to increase their understanding.

In a series of write-alouds, Ali thought out loud while she constructed a defense, an introduction, and a poem for her teacher multigenre writing project. She began by writing a poem to go along with her topic, children (see Figure 4.7). During that write-aloud she shared her thoughts about word choice, overall tone, the contribution it would make to her multigenre topic, the authenticity of the piece, the audience, and her purpose for writing it.

Once the poem was written, she went on to conduct a shared writing for the defense of the poem. She thought out loud about her knowledge of the purpose of the defense and how it should provide a thread that tied all the pieces together for continuity within the project. She wrote the following categories on the board: Genre; Characteristics of genre; Perspective; Audience; Why does this piece exist?; and Why did you write it? She then opened her personal writing journal and asked students to read her poem displayed on the overhead. Students discussed her poem and helped create the defense and thus created a dialogue about the construction of a defense. See Figure 4.8 for a partial transcript of this conversation.

FIGURE 4.7
Ali's Poem

Children are a work of art
Continually in progress
Happy to please
Hard to hurt
Open to all
Starving for knowledge
Willing to try
Content to play
Little babies
Aren't we all?

FIGURE 4.8
Conversation Surrounding Ali's Poem

ALI: You know how I keep a journal and I have a lot of writing pieces. I found this piece before school started and here is the poem I wrote. Thinking of who I am, what perspective is going to work for the defense?

TY: A poem.

ANTONIO: It could rhyme.

MAYA: You are the teacher and you are writing it.

ALI: Who is the audience?

KATIE: It was in your journal so you are the audience unless you get it published.

After all of her pieces were constructed, Ali demonstrated how to put together an introduction. She again thought out loud about how she wanted to introduce her multigenre writing project and what she wanted the reader to know about her as an author. She then involved the students in a conversation about the importance of the introduction and different ways that it could be constructed.

These write-alouds and think-alouds make thinking visible as they are shared with students. Just as we conduct think-alouds to demonstrate reading strategies, it is important to do the same with writing strategies that might at other times be lost to students. Think-alouds show students rather than tell them, which is important in constructing multigenre writing projects, when many students are taking risks as they create genres that are new and unfamiliar to them.

The whole-class lessons described previously are not in any chronological order but are interwoven throughout the multigenre writing project, and it is important to adapt the lessons to students' needs. These lessons therefore will occur at different times for different classrooms. It is important in a multigenre writing project to pre-plan lessons that will enhance students' understanding of multigenre writing, but it is also important to respond to the needs of students and to create lessons that build from their current understanding of genres and writing.

Similarly the small-group investigations occur in response to students' needs, and timing again will vary. Next we describe a variety of small-group investigations that scaffold students' understanding of genre and writing processes.

Small-Group Single-Genre Investigations

Small-group investigations focus more on constructing children's understanding of the genres they are writing. These groups help children negotiate genre definitions, read critically within a genre, and investigate similarities and differences across genres being investigated by students within the class.

Grouping by Genre

Once the proposals have been completed, construct a class chart of genres. Write each genre on the chart with the students' names underneath and a list of topics for easy reference. Students can refer to the chart to seek out classmates writing within the same genre for support. This is also an easy way to begin the small-group investigations. There are many ways to consider which groups to meet with first. A teacher might consider which group is the largest, which group is writing in a genre that is unfamiliar to all the students, or which group has the most struggling writers and therefore needs immediate support. Each classroom will be different and decisions should be made based on student needs and classroom management issues. If a large group of students are creating a genre that has been studied earlier in the year, they can use previous investigations to get them started. Every genre may not need an intense investigation. For example, making a list or creating a death certificate can be more of an independent study during which students rely on their knowledge of how to investigate genres established earlier in the year.

In whatever manner you choose to group students, the format for the group time is essentially the same. In the first meeting it is important to find out what the students already know about the genre and to discover the variety of purposes students describe for choosing each genre. This conversation is very interesting as children have very different reasons for choosing genres to go along with their topics. Within this meeting, the teacher provides guided reading experiences, as reading a variety of genres utilizes many reading strategies and approaches. Discussions also vary as students discuss the purpose of each genre.

In order to highlight how these meetings might go, we use an example from Suzette's classroom to describe the genre investigation of a brochure. In this particular class many students wanted to create a brochure for a variety of topics.

Exploration of Genre Samples

In the first meeting students brought their proposal and any examples of a brochure they had located. Suzette also brought in a plethora of genre samples from a variety of sources: businesses, vacations, products, classes to take, summer camps, theme parks, and so on. She was trying to meet the needs of all the writers in the group. The collection that children bring in is interesting in and of itself because it gives a teacher insight into what each child considers to be a great example of any particular genre. Consideration of where these samples come from is very important as the examples and students' background knowledge will construct the definition of the genre. So, it is important to have as wide a variety of samples as possible so as not to narrow the definition. Teachers must consider the many different ways the genre might be used or represented within their local community and try to represent a variety of perspectives, voices, and purposes for each genre.

Suzette placed the brochures on a table for the children to investigate. She listened to the children to get a sense of their understanding of the genre to make instructional decisions for future meetings. Once children had time to investigate, Suzette and the students created a chart listing some of the characteristics of a brochure, much like they did as a whole class for the single-genre study earlier in the year.

Shared or Guided Reading of Genre Examples

Once the students discuss some of the characteristics of the genre it is then important to support children's reading of the genre. Within this genre group there will be students with a variety of writing and reading abilities. All students can benefit from guided or shared reading of the genre. In order to facilitate this, make copies of a genre sample and give one to each student. Then discuss the language used—the format, structure, visuals, font, and point of view. Scaffold their understanding of the genre. It is important for students to read widely within their genre, especially if it happens to be their first experience with the genre.

Choose a sample of the genre that will help the whole group understand their genre. Suzette made copies of an amusement park brochure and a national parks brochure. She made copies of two different brochures because students were more familiar with the language in the amusement park brochure than they were with that in the national parks brochure; therefore, they needed to discuss the language at a deeper level for both brochures.

During the brochure guided reading, students first discussed how a reader would approach this text and what reading strategies would be most useful. For the amusement park brochure, students noticed that they previewed and skimmed the whole brochure first before reading the text. One student stated, "My eyes went to the pictures on the cover," and another noted, "The colors grabbed my attention." Students discussed the three-fold typical layout and how the brochure had informational boxes. They also noted that the language was persuasive like a commercial and contained expository elements as the brochure compared and contrasted other amusement parks. Suzette and the students then did a shared reading of a section of text from the national parks brochure and discussed the language.

This guided reading helps children focus on the particular reading strategies they will need to read and understand a particular genre. Even though there is great variance within any genre, the discussion supports readers as they keep their mentor text or choose a new one from the selection within the group. Once children read the selection they are then better able to enter into a critical discussion of the texts. In the brochure discussion, many students noticed the difference in texts and then thought about the audiences. This discussion led to a critical discussion of the genre.

Critical Reading of Genre

As it is important to discuss the many reading strategies that children need, it is equally important to ask particular questions of the text. These guiding questions help students think about a text at a deeper level. With each genre group a teacher could ask: Who is writing it? Who is the audience? What purpose does the genre have? What point of view is it written in? Is it effective? What if you changed this perspective? and Why would someone write this?

The critical discussion of the brochure helped children notice the many variances within a brochure genre, for example, the audience, the perspective, the purpose, and the group or individual writing it. Children broadened their understanding of what a brochure is, what it can do, and especially what it can't do. The following is a transcript of that conversation:

GRETA: It is like an advertisement; it persuades.
MARK: Yeah, it doesn't tell you all the information, just enough to get you to go or call for more information.
SHANTE: There are no personal thoughts like a diary entry.
ANTHONY: It will be very different for a sports team brochure. They will have to give scores and player information.
GRETA: That is just like the amusement park one; instead of getting you to go to the park, they want you to go to the game.

From this conversation it is easy to see that the children were getting a sense of the persuasive nature of brochures. Suzette was concerned that the children would think of the brochure only as persuasive in nature, so she found some other brochures from a local home improvement store that were of the how-to nature and were more informative. Students were then able to see that the elements were still very similar, but the text and illustrations changed to be more informative rather than persuasive.

What Does the Genre Bring to Your Topic?

Once the genre has been analyzed, it is important to bring the conversation back around to the students' multigenre writing projects as children need to answer what this genre brings to their topics. Students have a more expansive understanding of the genre now, so the teacher helps them articulate what this new information brings to their topics. Perhaps students see a new purpose to the genre or perhaps they would like to try it from a different perspective than first proposed. Students use their proposal to revise and expand their understanding and purpose of the genre. In some cases, children realize the genre looked like fun because their best friend was writing in this genre, but now they really can't make a case for it with their topic and need to find a more appropriate genre. This self-discovery is much more effective than a teacher just saying no!

During the brochure investigation several students realized there were many qualities of advertising and that this genre fit perfectly with their topics. Mark decided that his topic of automobiles needed brochures for the company and for particular cars; Greta decided that a brochure would help provide information about her topic, Anne Sullivan, so people would hire her for teaching; and Danny needed a brochure to advertise for Don McLean. However, Shante decided that a bumper sticker would be better for her topic, the seven wonders of the world, because she was not sure where she would hand brochures out. Finally, Mary reconsidered the brochure, as she thought a flyer would be a better avenue to advertise for her new dance studio (see Figure 4.9 for her finished flyer and Figure 4.10 for the brochure about Anne Sullivan).

Construction of Small-Group Genre Definition

After the intensive discussion and investigation of one particular genre, the group negotiates a definition of the genre and adds it to the list of characteristics they began at the beginning of the group meeting. This definition guides them through their own creation of text and provides common ground for all within the group to discuss their genre. Here's the definition Suzette's group came up with for the brochure:

> A text created to share information about a person, place, or thing. It can be persuasive or just give information. Many brochures can be colorful, but most of all they provide information sometimes on a folded piece of paper (tri-fold). They are easy to get to and easy to read, depending on the audience.

If students find other examples, they can add to the list and continue the conversation. Genre in these terms is defined by their experiences, their understanding of the genre in the world, and the examples brought into the classroom. Students need to understand that there is a broader definition of genre and that it is situated as part of a social process (Chapman 1999; Kress 1993). These genres have not always been out there to discover; they have been created and re-created to meet the needs of the writer and the intended audience. It is a difficult concept to help children understand, but they begin to understand it through the nature of the questions asked during the critical reading of the genre.

Each genre group goes through a similar process of discovery and expanding understanding. In each of these groups, the children are all writing within the same genre and have similar needs to create their writing pieces. After these meetings the teacher helps children decide how the information will influence their writing piece.

FIGURE 4.9
Mary's Dance Studio Flyer

COME CHECK US OUT!

Where: Dance Divas
           25 Bresson St.
           Summer, Oregon 89502

When: classes run between 1:00pm-10:00pm daily, except Sundays

Classes: Tap, Jazz, Ballet, Hip Hop, & Modern

Ages: 3yrs old - adults

About Us:

I am Michelle ████████, owner of Dance Divas. I've been a professional dancer for the past 20 years. I attended Julliard School of Dance for 10 years, and then was soon able to open my own dance school. We have 6 dance instructors. Their experiences are from recognized schools such as Julliard, Jeffery Ballet and Seffelen. In fact our instructors have performed in Cats, Christmas Carol, and Frankenstein. There is no better place for a dancer than DANCE DIVAS!

They might try some aspect in their writer's notebook or they might add to their goal sheet or begin or expand on their writing piece. However, as children engage in their writing, because of these small-group investigations, they all have similar language in which to discuss their writing pieces.

At other times it is important for children to get together in mixed genre groups to discuss and compare genres. The next section describes a series of whole-class small exploration groups. The teacher begins with instructions and then the class breaks up into small groups for a particular investigation. Three investigative groups are described—comparing genres, defining the purpose of a genre in the world, and analyzing how individual writing pieces add to the whole project.

Genre Comparison Groups

In groups that are comparing genres, students look closely at characteristics they have within their own writing. The purpose of this activity is to compare and contrast genres and their characteristics and then to help students add more depth or information to their own writing pieces. Students are grouped by genre, with either each

FIGURE 4.10
Brochure About Anne Sullivan

student in the group focusing on a different genre, or everyone working on the same genre. The teacher carefully constructs these groups to put particular genres together that have great comparative or contrasting elements or to place students in a group that will work well together. In either case, students compare and contrast a particular writing piece they are working on at the moment. Before entering the group, students list their genre on their own and define their genre on a genre comparison guide sheet. See Figure 4.11 for a sample guide sheet for teachers to use.

To begin, all students in a group share about their genre so students get an understanding of each different genre or share what they know about their common genre.

FIGURE 4.11
Genre Comparison Guide Sheet

Names:

Genre Study

Genre we're investigating:

Things that are unique to this type of writing:

Things about this genre that are similar to other types of writing:

Interesting characteristics that we should include in our own writing:

Then students investigate how their genre has unique characteristics that no other genre has and then consider similar characteristics across each genre. For instance, one student struggled with explaining what her PowerPoint piece was. She said, "It is not really like anything."

Tim replied, "PowerPoint shows information." The conversation continued as students tried to define a PowerPoint text. After a while Ali noticed this struggle and came over to help them understand that PowerPoint was just a mode of representation for their genre rather than a genre in itself. This struggle helped them realize they had a genre within their PowerPoint pieces.

Another group brought different genres to the meeting: a billboard; a radio broadcast interruption; an endangered species update; a sports newspaper article about a rookie of the month; and a letter to a bumper sticker production company (see Figure 4.12 for an example of the broadcast interruption and Figure 4.13 for the letter). In this meeting students shared their genres and during this discussion they realized all their examples used persuasive language. They were all trying to convince

FIGURE 4.12
Radio Broadcast Interruption

We interrupt this broadcast to warn you:

A creature has been spotted in the area. We suggest you lock your doors, windows, garage, and keep your children inside at all times. The monster has been sighted mainly at night in the Sun Valley area. No clear photographs or filming has been taken, but witnesses have reported piercing red eyes, a large figure, and clawed hands. This is no joke! I repeat this is no joke! More information will be provided as it comes in.

FIGURE 4.13
Letter to a Bumper Sticker Production Company

Mary
7769 High Street
West City, California 34567

June 4, 2005

Dance Bumper Sticker Manufacturer
1234 Dance Drive
New York, NY 1245

Dear Marketing Department:

I have created a bumper sticker that I believe will capture the interests of all dancers. I produced 50 bumper stickers, which I took to my dance class. Surprisingly, fellow dancers loved them so much that I only have five left. The dancers are putting them on their bedroom walls, lockers, notebooks, and their parents' car bumpers.

Since I am not able to produce these in large quantities I would like to sell my idea to you. We could make an agreement that would make both of us happy. Please call me at xxx-xxx-xxxx to discuss your interest in my bumper sticker. I have enclosed a copy of my bumper sticker for your review.

Sincerely,

Mary

people to do or buy something. Yet what was interesting is that they all had very different formats. Shante's billboard relied more on visual elements but the rest used texts with varied structures. Mary and Andrea wrote letters, Ty created a broadcast warning interruption, and John created a news article. Following are their lists of similarities and differences:

How are the genres unique?

❖ Different perspectives

❖ Different purpose for writing

❖ Audience

❖ Use of names in some

❖ Two use a lot of exclamation points

❖ Publishing is different—some are mailed some go in the paper and one is just read over the air

How are these genres similar?

❖ Persuasive language

❖ General audience

❖ Use of adjectives and descriptive language to persuade

❖ Does not provide any personal thoughts

Through this conversation the students discussed what a genre is and what it isn't. They also chatted about what it can and can't do.

At the end of this type of investigation it is important for students to think about how the activity can affect their writing. Each student fills in the bottom portion of her genre comparison guide sheet, which asks what characteristics could be included in the student's writing. For example, at the draft phase Mary decided to add a little more about how her dance students were using the bumper stickers; she thought that would add a more personal touch. Students then return to their writer's notebooks to reconsider their pieces.

Purpose of Genre in the World

In small-group meetings focused on the purpose of a genre in the world, students bring any piece they wish and they each ask one question to each other: Why does this piece exist? Students verbally defend the authenticity of their piece as they explain why someone or some organization would create the writing piece. They consider their topic as a whole and then defend to each other the necessity of the piece.

Lisa defended why someone would write a journal entry while traveling on the *Titanic*. She said, "It would be important to write down your ideas even before the iceberg hit because the ship was famous before that. Someone would keep a journal about each day on the trip." Katie was creating a multigenre writing project on herself and she defended why she would write a letter to a friend and write an autobiography. She simply stated, "I need to tell a friend why I like her and I need to remember about my tenth year of life."

These conversations also helped some think through their choices. Juan wanted to create a tombstone. (It was a popular genre in Suzette's class.) As he explained how he was creating a tombstone about a famous wrestler, students began to question the authenticity of his choice. "Why would you have a tombstone for someone who is alive?" He needed to defend that it was an imaginary piece and that if Bret Hart were no longer living, this is what his tombstone would say. He did not have to change his genre but he certainly had to explain why it might exist.

Students have a lot of fun with this inquiry as they are defending their choices verbally, and students ask a lot of questions of each other. Students at any phase of the writing process can enter into this conversation. Students can defend or explain a point of view or perspective, the setting of a piece, the audience, or the purpose. In this manner students have a conversation about the authenticity of the piece and defend the writerly choices they have made.

Analyzing Pieces and the Whole

In this last small-group inquiry, students refer back to an exercise we described in Chapter 3 in which students explored multigenre picture books. The investigation began with *The Jolly Postman* and continued with other multigenre picture books. In that activity students examined each genre but then looked at how each piece contributed to the whole. The new investigation builds from the knowledge gained while looking at the parts and considering how they related to the whole; students proceed with the same process but look at their own multigenre writing. Each student brings three or four drafts and explains his topic. The children then pair up and closely

FIGURE 4.14
Genre Guide Sheet

Analyzing Individual Genres and How They Add to the Whole

Title of piece:

Genre:

Voice:

Language:

Audience:

Point of view:

Who is telling the story?

Purpose of genre:

What does it add to the whole book?

What can this genre do that others cannot?

examine each other's multigenre writing projects using the genre guide sheet (see Figure 4.14). They examine how each genre contributes to the overall theme or topic.

Each student reads aloud her pieces and then the partners fill out the guide together. They then come back to the small group and discuss what they found out about each other's projects. See Figure 4.15 for a sample of a completed genre guide sheet.

Through the use of this guide sheet, Danny and Emily shared their insights about their pieces. In this discussion Emily and Danny noticed the variety of language used and how they each included elements of the time period for their particular topic— Ernest Shackleton during the early 1900s and Don McLean in the early 1970s. They described what each piece contributed. Emily's ABC book provided small fun facts about Ernest Shackleton and her letters were more of a personal nature, providing information about him and his wife. Danny's Don McLean buttons provided a visual of the much-used button fashion of the time. His brochure was a way to provide current information about the singer.

FIGURE 4.15
Completed Genre Guide Sheet

Analyzing Individual Genres and How They Add to the Whole

Title of piece: Letter to Queen

Genre: Letter

Voice formal and proper

Language: large words as I am writing to the Queen

Audience: Queen Elizabeth

Point of view: Ernest Shackleton

Who is telling the story?

Purpose of genre to thank the queen for knighting him.

What does it add to the whole book? His connection to the Queen gave a sense of his writing — added info about how he was knighted and

What can this genre do that the others can not? Share what he would write where he was to the Queen - other genres cannot show them talking.

This activity provided a way for students to articulate how each piece provided a layered effect on their information, topic, or theme. Emily's multigenre project on Ernest Shackleton created a wide spectrum of information and each piece contributed something the other pieces could not. Emily stated,

> The ABC book gives facts about his life, and the letters tell you about how he was feeling and some things about his wife. The recruitment flyer used words he might have used during the time as he used similar words to describe the journey and the job. None of the pieces say that, you need all of the pieces to tell his story.

All the small-group activities are completed during the drafting phases of the multigenre writing project. In this manner students are able to revise and refine their writing pieces as new insights are gained based on the conversations and explorations of their own pieces as well as those of their classmates. After each small-group investigation, the teacher gives students time to write so they can incorporate any revision to enhance their writing pieces. During any of these activities, the room is filled with talk of writing, purpose, audience, perspective, and most of all genres.

In the next section we describe how the teacher can scaffold and conference with students about their individual writing pieces. These teacher-student conferences are at the heart of the multigenre writing project. The teacher acts as a bridge between small-group and whole-class activities and students' individual understanding of their writing projects.

Individual Conferences

During writing workshop time, students are drafting and constructing their multigenre pieces. Writing workshop options are very similar to those described in Chapter 2. Students research, read, and write drafts of their writing pieces. During this time the teacher attends individual conferences. Conferences occur in three ways: student request, teacher request, or roaming around the room and having conferences with students on the spot. With student-requested conferences, students come prepared to describe the kind of help they need. During roaming conferences, the teacher allows the student to take the lead and asks, "How's it going?"

These conferences for the most part are not any different than those described by Wood Ray (2001) or Fletcher and Portalupi (2001). In these wonderfully descriptive books the authors describe how these conferences are used to keep the writing going and to support the child at the point when she needs help the most, in the act of writing. Conferences during the multigenre writing project take the same stance. However, there are conferences that are little different due to the nature of the project. A few of these are described here.

How's It Going?

In roaming conferences, the teacher and student check the progress of all pieces: defenses, introduction, and visual elements. The teacher asks the student to take out all pieces, proposal, and time line. Together they discuss the management of the pieces, how they all fit into the whole, and what struggles the student is having with any one piece. During this meeting the teacher will certainly suggest ways to manage all four pieces of writing at one time. In the following dialogue, Suzette was conferencing with Katie, who was off task because someone else was using the computer.

SUZETTE: So what could you work on right now instead of your PowerPoint?
KATIE: I could work on my song, bumper sticker, or news report.
SUZETTE: What do you need to do for your song?
KATIE: I need to research and get ideas.
SUZETTE: Is that a good option for you for today?
KATIE: Yep.
SUZETTE: OK, let me know if you need help.

Katie then took out three books she had checked out from the library, read through them, and then took out her writer's notebook to work on her draft of a song.

In another conference Suzette was discussing management issues with Anthony. He was having trouble keeping track of all his pieces. She helped him to organize his draft notebook and helped him remove any items that were not related to writing. She also had him open his portfolio folder and remove any writing pieces he had stored in his desk. Together they came up with a plan to keep his work organized and safe.

Teachers need to help students with writing as well. It is important to support children's effort to create a unified whole with the entire multigenre paper. The teacher conferences about voice and audience as well as to negotiate how a piece sounds in respect to the audience the student has identified as important.

Drafting a Piece

The teacher should be available to students as they are writing their pieces. Drafting conferences keep in mind the project as a whole. As a teacher meets with a student, they consider the piece and how it will add to the whole project.

In the partial transcript in Figure 4.16 Emily had requested a conference with her teacher, Suzette. She wanted to create an ABC book for Ernest Shackleton (see Figure 1.1) but was having trouble getting started. In this conference Suzette and Emily attended to the questions on her proposal. Even though she had already completed her proposal and investigated ABC books, Emily was still unsure of how to get started.

Audience

Audience is a very important element within any writing piece. The audience helps the writer to structure the piece and choose language that is appropriate for the intended audience. Many times children lose sight of their intended audience and their writing takes on a generic tone, or the audience needs to be reconsidered, as in the following conference between Ali and Anna. Anna wanted to create a bumper sticker to try to persuade people to stop making graffiti. Her understanding of her audience was faulty.

ANNA: Which bumper sticker should I do?

ALI: What is the purpose of the bumper sticker?

ANNA: To keep people from doing graffiti.

ALI: Who is the audience?

ANNA: Gang members.

ALI: The audience is gang members, hmmm. . . . Do you think they will buy this bumper sticker?

ANNA: Uhhh, maybe not.

ALI: What organization gets rid of graffiti?

ANNA: Maybe police and school agencies.

SUZETTE:	Let's look at the characteristics of an ABC book and make a checklist.
EMILY:	They have pictures and words that go with the letter. They are not as exciting because they just go with the letter.
SUZETTE:	Yes, an ABC book usually has one page per letter.
EMILY:	They have definitions, brief definitions. They should be easy to read for young children.
SUZETTE:	Are ABC books fiction or nonfiction?
EMILY:	Usually nonfiction. You could make a fictional one like Dr. Seuss.

FIGURE 4.16
Emily and Suzette's Conference

FIGURE 4.17
Anna's Bumper Stickers

ALI: Where would you market this bumper sticker? What if you did a fund-raiser and did an antigang campaign? Who will buy and sell these stickers?

ANNA: Grocery stores, maybe police would help distribute ideas. So there are really two audiences. I want gang members to stop tagging, but I need to sell it to people like me who want it to stop. OK I can write now.

See Figure 4.17 for Anna's bumper stickers. In this conference Ali helped Anna to think through the importance of audience and how her word choice would need to be appropriate for her intended audience.

Authenticity of Piece

Following that conference on audience, Anna then proceeded to research possible authentic audiences for her bumper sticker. She found an organization called GREAT—Gang Resistance Education and Teaching. It was a local antigang organization that worked at getting children out of gangs and stopping graffiti in her neighborhood. She asked her teacher to help her understand what the organization was and what it did and if it would be a good group to send her bumper sticker to. Anna and Ali worked together to help her business letter to the organization seem authentic and to make sure the perspective of her piece would be appropriate.

These conferences about audience and perspective take on many shapes, but keeping the writers' focus on these elements helps them to structure their piece in an effective manner. Getting a feel for these conferences is imperative as each student is creating different genre pieces on different topics.

The Unified Whole

As publishing time draws near, many of the conferences focus on putting it all together. Teacher and student look at all the pieces—defense, introduction, table of contents, and genres—and make decisions as to the order of the project. The teacher also reviews pieces with each student to ensure the multigenre writing project is a unified whole. Teacher and student read through the pieces and determine whether the introduction provides enough background information for the reader to enjoy and understand his project. Many times these conferences contain two or three students and the teacher engages in discussion about how best to put the project together.

In these conferences students place their entire writing project on a table and read and discuss each piece. The teacher asks questions like:

❖ What is the most important theme in your project?

❖ What piece demonstrates this idea?

❖ Do you want to open or close with this piece?

❖ Which pieces will help the reader to understand another piece?

❖ Which order should they go in?

❖ Does your introduction help the reader understand your project?

❖ Tell me more about why you chose that order.

These guiding questions help students to think about each piece at a deeper level. Students must be cognizant of their choices and the structure of their multigenre writing project.

After these conferences the students put it all together into a multigenre writing package. Usually these projects are bound with project covers or published and shown through some multimedia display. The intricate publishing decisions really come with the individual pieces; however, the whole package is important as well for the reader to understand the project as a whole presentation rather than separate writing pieces bound by a common cover.

Publishing Ideas

There are many publishing options. One important aspect to consider when publishing multigenre writing projects is authenticity. Students spend much of their time considering the authenticity of a writing piece as they ask and answer the question Why does this piece exist? As they answer this question they defend why someone would write within this particular genre, what it would look like in the real world, and who is going to be reading it. For example, in Julie's project on an engineer, she created a journal written from Leonardo da Vinci's perspective. She wrote it on the computer and used a cursive font and blanched paper, and she had the computer write the entries backward because da Vinci often wrote in code.

Students have found many creative ways to publish their pieces and to make them seem *and* to be authentic pieces of writing. Many use PowerPoint to present their writing as commercials or reports. These multimedia presentations are very effective and can be used like a storyboard design; often children incorporate Internet sites and create links to enhance their genre. For example, Joe created a quiz show for his multi-genre writing project on stars. He used PowerPoint to set up the question design and then had links to Internet sites that provided the answers. He created a sort of electronic game show. Another student, Michael, created commercials through PowerPoint and used the visual effects and links as a persuasive tactic.

Other students, like Lisa, realize that a more traditional publication is needed to be more authentic. She stated:

> The journal entries from the *Titanic* survivor would be old and therefore would need to be written in cursive and on old paper to make it seem real. If I used PowerPoint I would have to change the perspective and be a researcher of the *Titanic*, then using the computer would seem real.

For these students, publishing decisions were based on the time and perspective of the piece as well as the audience.

Sharing Projects and Celebrating

So much work goes into these projects that a celebration and sharing of the projects seems natural. Many students like to set up a museum of their work. At their desks or tables they set out their multigenre writing pieces and books or references they have used to provide a sort of journey for the reader. In Ali's classroom students spent an entire morning rotating around the room and reading each student's project. She created a form for students to use so they could give comments and feedback on each student's project (see Figure 4.18). Once students rotated around the room, she gathered them in a circle and they ate and drank and discussed the successes and what they noticed in each other's projects. She also asked them how she could improve the project.

In Suzette's classroom all parents, friends, and administrators are invited in to read and discuss the multigenre writing projects. Parents are informed well in advance so they can make arrangements to come in. Students and their parents rotate around the room, reading each other's projects. In this case both students and parents provide feedback on a sheet of paper for the writer.

After all the projects have been read, they too enjoy snacks and gather on the floor to discuss the projects. The parents offer their perspectives on writing and the projects as well. Suzette takes notes and reflects on the process as a whole.

In whatever manner a teacher chooses to celebrate and share, the most important aspect is the reading of the projects. They can be shared with reading buddies, other classrooms, or the principal of the school, or even placed in a school newsletter or newspaper. Multigenre projects need to be shared and celebrated.

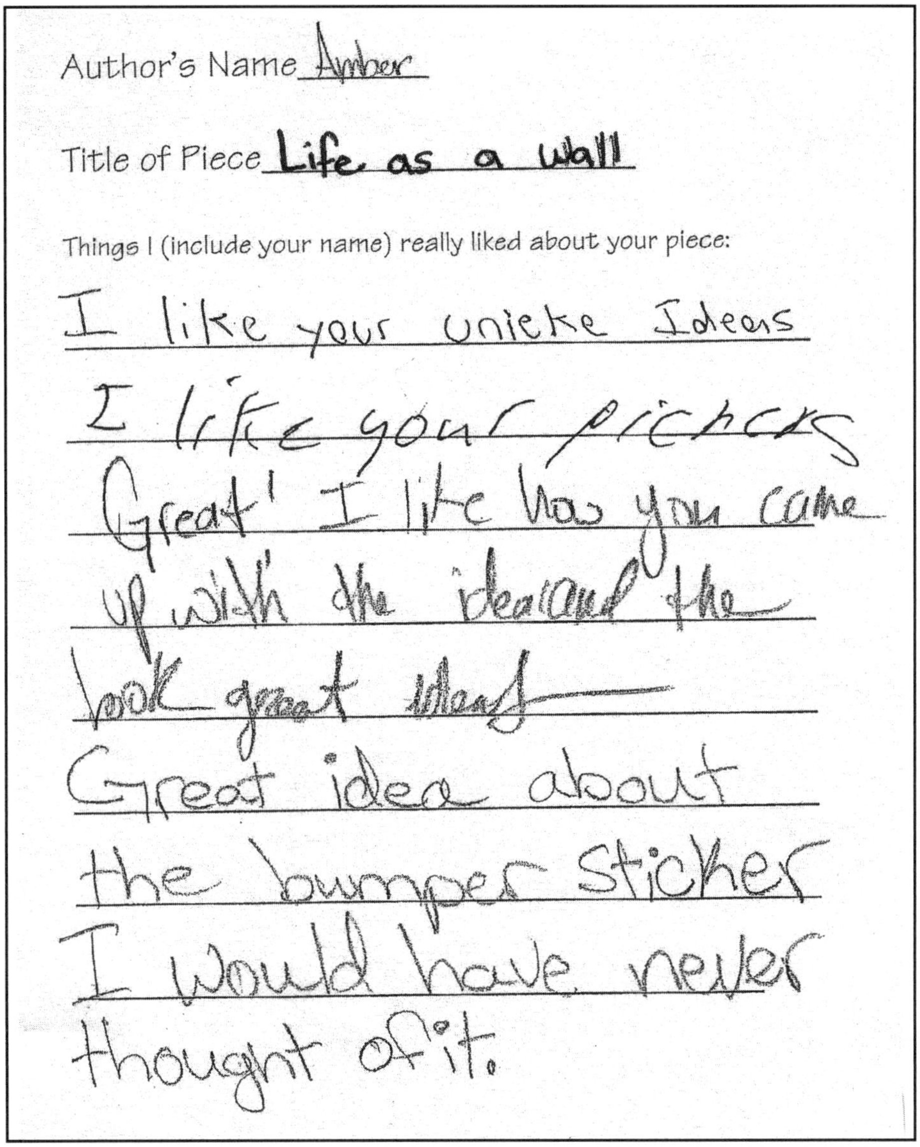

FIGURE 4.18
Comment Form

Author's Name Amber

Title of Piece **Life as a Wall**

Things I (include your name) really liked about your piece:

I like your unieke Ideas

I like your pichers

Great! I like how you came

up with the idea and the

book great idea

Great idea about

the bumper sticker

I would have never

thought of it.

This chapter highlights a more typical approach to multigenre writing, from a research or rather a personal choice approach. In the next chapter we highlight alternatives to this approach. The study of genre and writing is still at the heart of the project, but we demonstrate other ways to enter into multigenre writing and how it can be approached in the primary classroom as well.

References

Chapman, M. 1999. "Situated, Social, Active: Rewriting Genre in the Elementary Classroom." *Written Communication* 16 (4): 469–90.

Fletcher, R., and J. Portalupi. 2001. *The Writing Workshop: The Essential Guide.* Portsmouth, NH: Heinemann.

Graves, D. 2003. *Why Write with Students?* Annual Conference of the National Council of Teachers of English, San Francisco, CA.

Kress, G. 1993. "Genre as Social Process." In *The Powers of Literacy: A Genre Approach to Teaching Writing,* ed. B. Cope and M. Kalantzis, 22–37. Pittsburgh: University of Pittsburgh Press.

Serafini, F., and S. Sarafini Youngs. 2006. *Around the Reading Workshop in 180 Days.* Portsmouth, NH: Heinemann.

Wood Ray, K. 2001. *The Writing Workshop: Working through the Hard Parts (And They're All Hard Parts).* Urbana, IL: NCTE.

CHAPTER 5

Units of Study and Multigenre Writing

In her early years of teaching multigenre writing, Suzette did not begin from a research paper approach; instead she looked at what already existed in her curriculum and found ways to use multigenre writing to expand students' understanding of historical figures and events. She felt it was important to begin slowly and add on to her already existing units of study. She asked herself, "Where in my curriculum would multigenre writing fit? And what units of study already exist that would lend themselves to multigenre writing?"

In the previous chapters we outlined a typical approach to multigenre writing, meaning it follows in many ways the descriptions of multigenre writing by Tom Romano (2000), Camille Allen (2001), and Melinda Putz (2006). In this chapter we move from Suzette's curricular quest and expand the repertoire of multigenre writing and describe ways of entering into this type of writing from a more direct connection to existing curriculum units of study.

Multigenre writing has historically been presented as an alternative to the traditional research paper, but it can also enhance existing units of study. In this chapter we outline four units of study in which multigenre writing is a powerful extension to students' understanding of topic and genre. The first unit of study is a persuasive speech unit with a focus on historical figures and biography; the second is a unit of study focusing on biography in the primary grades; the third is a unit on the Revolutionary War; and the fourth is a focus on multigenre writing as a response to literature.

Balloon Speech (Biography and Persuasive Writing)

This unit of study spans across the reading and writing workshop as well as into the social studies curriculum. It is an in-depth study of historical events and people as well as a study of persuasive writing, research, debate skills, public speaking, and multigenre writing. Another description of this unit can also be found in *Around the Reading Workshop in 180 Days* (Serafini and Serafini Youngs 2006). In this unit students are asked to choose a historical figure and research him or her in depth.

This is the scenario students receive:

> Choose a person real or fictional to become. You will research this person in depth and become this person in every way possible. Then imagine you are stranded on a deserted island and there is only one way off the island: a balloon that will take you and four other people to another island where one final balloon is waiting for you. This balloon will carry only one person back to civilization. In

order to be the sole survivor, you must convince a panel of people (the audience the night of the speeches) that you are the most important and influential person in the world. You must convince the audience that you should be the one to survive. If you do not survive, you and all of your contributions to the world will never have existed at all.

You will write a five-minute speech to convince the audience that who you are and all your contributions are so important that you must be the sole person to get back to civilization. You will research the other people in your balloon and use that information in a debate against your balloonmates to decide who the most important person is. You will give your speech and have one minute for rebuttal, the audience will vote, and a balloon winner will be declared. Good luck!

The unit begins with a two-week in-depth search for just the right person. Students and teacher venture to the local library for research materials and interview parents and other family members and friends to get personal reactions to the historical figures they are considering. Here is a sampling of the people children have chosen over the years.

Thomas Jefferson	Abigail Adams	FDR
Ben Franklin	Oprah Winfrey	Rudolph Giuliani
George Washington	Santa Claus	John Elway
Abraham Lincoln	Celine Dion	Rosa Parks
Henry Ford	Sojourner Truth	George W. Bush
Albert Einstein	J. K. Rowling	a child
Bill Clinton	a mom	Jane Goodall
Bill Gates	Hillary Clinton	Alexander Graham Bell
Don McLean	Amelia Earhart	Lance Armstrong
NYC firefighter	Suzan B. Anthony	Walt Disney
JFK	Rachael Carson	Joan of Ark
Gandhi	Princess Diana	Anne Frank
Leonardo da Vinci	Harriet Tubman	Diane Fossey
Martin Luther King Jr.	an engineer	Chuck Yeager
J. R. R. Tolkien	a teacher	Clara Barton
Jim Carrey	Mother Teresa	Sadako
Ernest Shackleton	Anne Sullivan	Vincent van Gogh
Mickey Mouse	Eve	Galileo
the Devil	Shirley Temple	Elvis
the Grim Reaper	Easter Bunny	Teddy Roosevelt
Jesus	a pediatrician	Madam Curie
Dr. Charles Drew	Mother Nature	Helen Keller
Dalai Lama	Lance Burton	Mozart
Coretta Scott King	Christopher Reeves	
Ruby Bridges	God	

Once each student chooses her person, the teacher collects the names and places them into a hat. The teacher then pulls out five names at a time to form balloon groups. Students are very eager to form groups as it sets their research agenda and they then know the identities of their competitors. The teacher begins a series of lessons on research skills, critical reading, persuasive writing, public speaking, and debate skills.

Single-Genre Study: Persuasive Writing

All efforts are placed on a common genre—a persuasive speech. The teacher provides a sample outline for students to follow. It has particular required sections but the order is up to the student. Students must include an opening; pertinent background information including childhood, schooling, and adult life; at least five contributions to society; research information on the other four members of their group; a closing; and a prepared rebuttal. All students begin with the same genre but focus on different times in history and current events. Their speech is written in the first person and tells the life of their person. Students spend two weeks researching their historical figure and their opponents' figures. Students have the option of switching back and forth from opponents to their own figure, giving them some freedom during the writing workshop time.

For some students it is a daunting task to research four or five people, so investigative groups are formed to give support to their research efforts. In this group, four students team up and research the other opponent, plan a team effort, and divide up the information for their speeches. Students rotate until all figures have been researched. They are all sworn to secrecy, as they do not want the other person to know what information they have found out about his figure. For example, in one group Harriet Tubman, Santa Claus, and Ernest Shackleton worked together to research Hillary Clinton. Once they completed their research and divided the information, then Hillary Clinton, Santa Claus, and Harriet Tubman worked together to research Ernest Shackleton, and the rotation continued until all opponents had been researched.

In many cases it is not about finding negative attributes but rather about comparing major contributions and weighing the impact the contributions had on society. Students look closely at historical, world, and current events and compare the effects and impact each person has had on society. The writing of the speech is based on a person's contribution but students also have an understanding of the impact of the historical events of the time as well.

The unit of study at this point is very similar to any genre study, as described in Chapter 2. Students are exposed to a variety of examples of persuasive speeches, they explore and critically read and watch videos of the contents of these speeches, and then they begin to experiment with their own persuasive speech writing. Students spend about a month in preparation for the balloon speeches. They research their person, investigate (dig up the dirt, as Suzette's students like to call it) their opponents, practice impromptu speeches, create an outline, and then write their speech and experiment with various openings and closings to their speech.

As students prepare their speech, they begin to see their person from a variety of perspectives. They understand the major contributions he or she has made, but they also understand mistakes their person has made and to try and defend them and explain why their person might have done what he or she did. They also understand how other historical figures and characters might have perceived their person's actions. Not only do students write from their perspective and create arguments against their opponents, but also they must predict what their opponents might say about them. What arguments would come from these other perspectives? Using the earlier example, they need to think: What would Ernest Shackleton, Santa Claus, and Harriet Tubman say about Hillary Clinton? The information gathered is then used in their argument or rebuttal section.

By considering these multiple perspectives on their historical figure, students have a true advantage when it comes to the multigenre writing project, as they can imagine what writing this person might do and what writing might have been created about him or her. In order to prepare for the speech they need to predict what another historical figure might say and imagine how their figure's actions would be perceived. In many cases the balloons are filled with figures from different time periods and sometimes the figures are from a fictional world. Here are some of the groupings that have occurred in Suzette's classroom over the years.

Group 1	Group 2	Group 3
Sojourner Truth	a teacher	Easter Bunny
J. K. Rowling	Albert Einstein	a mom
George Washington	Thomas Jefferson	Santa Claus
Rudolph Giuliani	Thomas Edison	a pediatrician

Group 4	Group 5
Mickey Mouse	Christopher Reeves
Martin Luther King Jr.	God
Gandhi	FDR
Mother Nature	Spongebob Squarepants
Lance Burton	

On the night of the speeches, parents, friends, and family attend the big event. Each student gives a speech and then takes notes on the other speeches to prepare for her one-minute rebuttal. After students have given their speeches, they each have one minute to say something in defense of what has been said about their figure, a new point to consider or a reminder of their person's major contributions. There are five to seven rounds of speeches. At the end of each balloon group, the audience votes. At the end of all the rounds, the winners are announced and then a dinner break occurs to allow the finalists time to prepare for their final speeches. At the end of the evening a winner is declared (see Figure 5.1 for an excerpt of a Mother Teresa speech).

FIGURE 5.1
Excerpt from Mother Teresa Speech

What gives you the greatest joy in life? To me it is seeing a homeless child laugh or to hear a dying man's last words be "thank you" because we rescued him from the streets. To find out how I (Mother Teresa) came to rescue children and dying men and women we have to go many years back to my childhood. I was born in Skopje, Yugoslavia. I had an older brother and sister... I love to give children a smile and to be their friend so I started homes for abandoned children.

From Persuasive Writing to Multiple Genres

Once the speeches are completed students begin to consider multiple genres from their person's perspective. They consider genres that would have been appropriate for their person and they consider the perspective and who should be writing the piece. Students understand so much about their historical person that typically they focus their research efforts on investigating possible genres. Students keep their resources so they have a quick reference once they begin to write if further research is necessary.

The teacher brainstorms possible genres with the students. In a class discussion students share the kinds of writing each historical person created and the impact the writing had on society. In many cases it is very obvious, such as Martin Luther King Jr.'s *I Have a Dream* speech; Abigail Adams' letters to John Adams; Thomas Jefferson's writings and contribution to the Constitution; and Hillary Clinton's speeches as first lady and as senator. In other cases it is more difficult, and students need to imagine what writing or speeches the Grim Reaper might give, for example, or what Mickey Mouse might write. Students who want to write through more modern genres like a PowerPoint presentation, a web page, or a magazine article need only to consider the perspective and think authentically about who might create a genre *about* their person.

The talk in the classroom during this time is about finding the most authentic pieces of writing that a historical person would have created or someone would have created about the person. All students are entering into the multigenre writing from the same perspective, as the persuasive speech is the foundation of their project.

Small-Group Investigations

Investigative groups can be formed based on the time period each person is from, common causes and contributions, or common and different genres. The biography focus allows a teacher to investigate genres and people as they connect to other historical or fictional characters because of the nature of the multigenre writing. As students prepare their rebuttal and argument, they are connecting historical and fictional characters in unique ways. The scenario of placing characters pulled from different time periods on an island allows students to make connections to other characters and the conversations they might have. This understanding of historical figures is in depth as they are able to apply their understanding out of the context of a particular time period.

Investigating Time Period

Each student creates his own time line of his person, choosing which historical events are most pertinent. Figure 5.2 showcases part of a time line for the Dalai Lama. Then, on the board or on chart paper, the class creates one large time line and places all the individual historical time lines on it.

To clarify time periods, each person can be a different color. This gives the class an understanding of each person in history and creates a visual representation of the time period when these historical people were the most influential. Students are placed into small groups based on the time line and overlapping dates. If too many students are in one time period, then it will be necessary to form a few smaller groups. In this manner students discuss the major events of the time period

FIGURE 5.2
Time line for the Dalai Lama

Dalai Lama Time Line

1935 The Dalai Lama was born in the province of Amdo near the Chinese border.

1938 The Tibetan government sent a search party and found the Dalai Lama. He is taken to Lhasa the capital of Tibet.

1940 The Dalai Lama was taken to Poltala Palace and proclaimed the official Dalai Lama. He was then educated at a monastery in Lhasa.

1950 The Chinese start to invade. They take over the Amdo and others near border provinces. The Chinese use their military power to take over all of Tibet in the next 9 years. They torture people and systematically take over.

FIGURE 5.3
Time Period Genre Discussion Guide

Time Period Genre Discussion Guide

Time Period: From year_____ to year _____

Genres used by your historical person:

_____   _____
_____   _____
_____   _____
_____   _____

Genres typical for that time period:

_____   _____
_____   _____
_____   _____
_____   _____

Genres you might like to try:

_____   _____
_____   _____
_____   _____
_____   _____

and the kinds of writing and public speaking that were common during that time. Students are given a guide sheet to help them begin this type of discussion (see Figure 5.3). At first the discussion is on major events in history rather than genre, but that is just a way of grouping. Once the groups are formed, students begin to discuss historical genres.

During the discussion of historical genres students share information gained during the research phase and share with each other the genres used by their historical figure and genres from the time period that each student discovered. For example, Figure 5.4 shows a completed time period guide on Abigail Adams.

Lauren's historical figure was Abigail Adams and as can be seen by her completed guide sheet, she was familiar with Abigail's letters to her husband, John Adams.

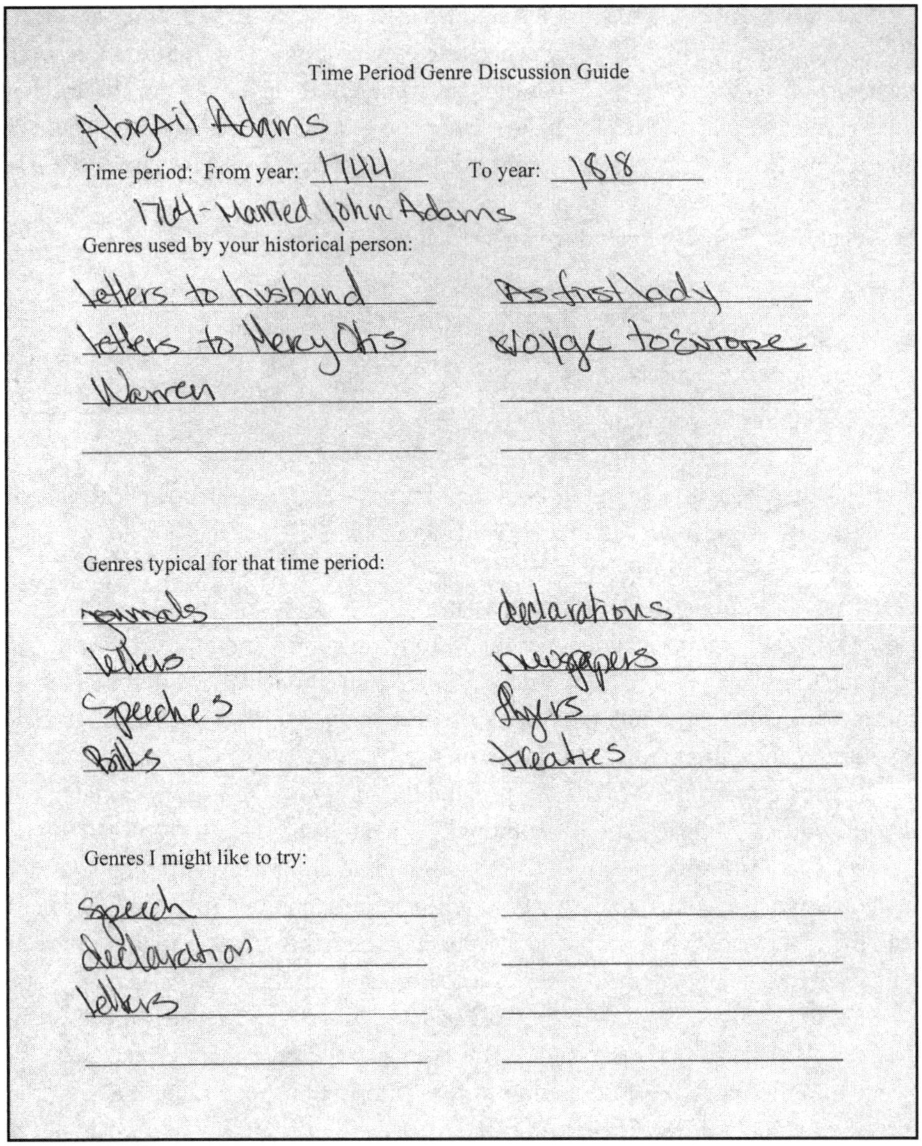

FIGURE 5.4
Time Period Genre Guide on
Abigail Adams

Time Period Genre Discussion Guide

Abigail Adams

Time period: From year: 1744   To year: 1818

1744- Married John Adams

Genres used by your historical person:

letters to husband   As first lady

letters to Mercy Otis   voyage to Europe

Warren

Genres typical for that time period:

journals   declarations

letters   newspapers

speeches   flyers

bills   treaties

Genres I might like to try:

speech

declaration

letters

Lauren wanted her writing to be authentic and so in this group, the students discussed the role of women during that time period. She needed this understanding to
help her imagine other genres Abigail might use authentically. Following is part of
their conversation:

LAUREN: Abigail wrote letters to her husband. What if she wrote them to other
people?

HEATHER: Who would she write to?

JOHN: Other women.

LAUREN: Why only women?

JOHN: Other men are not going to read her letters and if they do they are not
going to take her seriously because she is a woman.

HEATHER: Yeah, Martha Washington was expected to give parties and to receive
guests, not really make major decisions.

The purpose of discussion in these groups is to investigate what genres are available and for students to discover which genres could communicate information about their person most effectively. When groups complete their discussion, the teacher meets with the whole class to discuss what the students discovered during these group conversations. The teacher might ask:

❖ What new genres did you discover?

❖ How did the time period impact the genres?

❖ Are there genres that span across all time periods?

❖ What genres are specific to the time period?

❖ What genres do you want to try?

Students then have time to think about their proposal and to write down ideas about new and interesting genres in their writer's notebook.

Common Causes and Contributions

Another way to organize students for brainstorming genres and topics for writing is to group them by their figures' contributions. On a sheet of chart paper, list all of the causes and major contributions made by each person. Then have the class discuss ways to organize the groups. This is an interesting discussion to have as they make connections across time periods. For example, during one discussion, students felt that Sojourner Truth, Susan B. Anthony, Lucretia Mott, Oprah Winfrey, Hillary Clinton, and Abraham Lincoln should be in the same group because they fought for the equal rights of women and African Americans. Through their discussion they realized that the means these people had to pursue their fights for equal rights were not equal due to time period, gender, power position (status), and financial status.

How to group is a very interesting and powerful discussion to have with children. Again they begin to understand historical events in a deeper manner but they also begin to understand the time period and as efforts transcend time, they see the threads of contributions of people in earlier times.

During these groups students begin the conversation around major contributions and then they discuss the genres used as avenues to reach and persuade other citizens. To facilitate this conversation, the teacher uses a guide sheet for this small-group investigation (see Figure 5.5). Each student fills out her own sheet and uses the information from the discussion to make decisions for the multigenre writing project. For an example of a completed form on Oprah Winfrey, see Figure 5.6.

These small-group investigations take about a week to complete. During this time students are given a multigenre writing proposal and asked to consider four to seven more pieces to write, depending on the time available. The proposal is similar to the one in Chapter 3 except the topic explanation is eliminated. Students focus their attention on the genres and describe the authenticity of their pieces, once again answering the question—Why does this piece exist?

Genre Groups

Once students have completed their proposal and are ready to begin drafting, genre groups are formed in the same way as described in Chapter 4. Students meet with the

FIGURE 5.5
Major Contribution Discussion Guide

Major Contribution Discussion Guide

Name:

Major Contributions:

1.

2.

3.

4.

5.

Genres used:

What other genres could this person have used?

What genres will help the reader to get a complete understanding of this person and his or her contributions to society?

---

teacher and preview many examples; explore the genres with critical reading; and experiment with their own writing. Depending on need, the teacher can group students based on common genres or have them investigate similarities and differences among genres. Students then revise, edit, and publish their multigenre writing projects (see Figure 5.7 for a fourth-grade example of a completed multigenre writing project centered on Ben Franklin).

Parents are invited to the celebration, as they are eager to see the expansion on students' understanding of their historical figures since the night of their presentation of the balloon speeches. Multigenre writing projects are shared with reading buddies and administrators who would like to attend the celebration.

In the next section we present another biography unit of study, for primary-grade students. Students begin with writing a biography and then venture into writing two pieces and creating a visual element to extend their writing.

FIGURE 5.6
Major Contribution Discussion Guide on Oprah Winfrey

Major contribution discussion guide

Name: Oprah Winfrey

Major contributions:
1. power position for African American woman
2. talk show for people to get help
3. give away many things
4. bring awareness to important topics
5. promotes reading

Genres used:
speech   talk show
recipes
books
journal
letters

What other genres could this person have used?
inyral adress
memories
picture book
recipe book

What genres will help the reader to get a complete understanding of this person and their contributions to society?

ABC book
journal entries from people she's helped
tv show
letters from family on childhood

Primary Focus on Biography

In the primary grades it almost seems natural to use multigenre writing, as the children are eager to learn about various ways to write. As teachers engage students in their first research projects, they spend considerable energy showing students the places to search for information, how to represent it, and how to prepare a report for others to read. Once these reports are complete, teachers often move on to another research report topic. We are suggesting that before such a move, teachers allow students to build on their knowledge about a topic and expand their report into a multigenre project. The teacher can capitalize on students' knowledge of the topic and expand their writing repertoires and venture into other genres that connect to the person or topic. The routines are essentially the same as those engaged in by intermediate students. Teachers may just need to scaffold the projects a bit more. For instance, they may need to be more explicit about each genre possibility that they model for students.

One way to enter into multigenre writing is to move from a single-genre study of biography in the primary grades to a multigenre project. For example, students in first-, second-, and third-grade classrooms were studying about important figures in history. Their teacher provided numerous books and other resources for students to

FIGURE 5.7
Ben Franklin Project

Oct. 9, 1715

Dear Friend,

I apologize for what happened today. I know you had your opinions, and I had mine, and I'm sorry your opinion was undoubtedly wrong.

It is absurd to think that wind is created inside the clouds. It is only too obvious that wind is formed far above earth by the wings of many birds.

Wind is strong enough to move the clouds, for if the wind came from the cloud itself the cloud would be propelled in the opposite direction of the cloud. However, a cloud travels with the wind, not against it.

I'm sure you're on the right track now, unless you've got evidence to prove me wrong. If so, please write back!

Your friend,

Ben Franklin

May 10, 1775

Another negotiation meeting down the drain. You would think that the stupid people would stop charging us so much for tea. What's the deal here, I mean why shouldn't we have our independence, why are we being taxed for things like the wood we chop for our own houses? If war ever breaks out, which I am sure it will, how will we defend ourselves? It would take everyone here to fight their army, I don't even want to think about it....

Ben's Haiku Poem

Hear the frightening sound
The thunder is almighty
Stay out of its way!

Wow, what a big storm
Hey, is that a kite up there?
Boom, crash, oh poor Ben!

Here little kitty,
Stay indoors till the storm's through
Zap! Well I warned you!

explore. Their first activity was to write a traditional report about their person. In Figure 5.8 is second grader Chandler's writing about Ruby Bridges. Her report includes important facts and also some personal opinion, such as where she writes about Ruby "being lucky." Building from this report are a couple of samples from her multigenre project on Ruby Bridges. The first multigenre example is a letter (see Figure 5.9) written to Ruby from Sally. Chandler provided an introduction to her letter that explained who the letter was from. A final sample is an excerpt from Ruby's journal that allowed the reader to experience Ruby's feelings (see Figure 5.10).

This sample project provides evidence that multigenre writing is an appropriate vehicle for even the youngest writers. Through its use, young children understand various genres and how they can work together to enrich classroom study.

FIGURE 5.8
Chandler's Biography of Ruby Bridges

Ruby Bridges

I'm learning about Ruby Bridges, a little girl who was very brave. She was born in 1954 in Tylor or missippi.

There were many facts about Ruby that made her a famous American as a child. She was in the classroom all alone. She was the first black girl to go to an all white school.

She helped others. The police had to drive her to school.

Revolutionary War Multigenre Writing Projects

There are countless places within the curriculum where multigenre writing can be used to expand students' understanding of topic and genre. It is exciting to think of the possibilities for this kind of writing. Students and teacher can engage in an in-depth study of history or science and then use multigenre writing as a culminating experience to the unit. This kind of writing requires students to think about history or science topics from a variety of perspectives and to imagine ways to express their understanding of science and social studies concepts.

We would like to share with you one example of a Revolutionary War unit conducted in Suzette's and Ali's fifth-grade classrooms. The objectives for the unit were for students to understand the dates and major events surrounding the start, dura-

FIGURE 5.8
(continued)

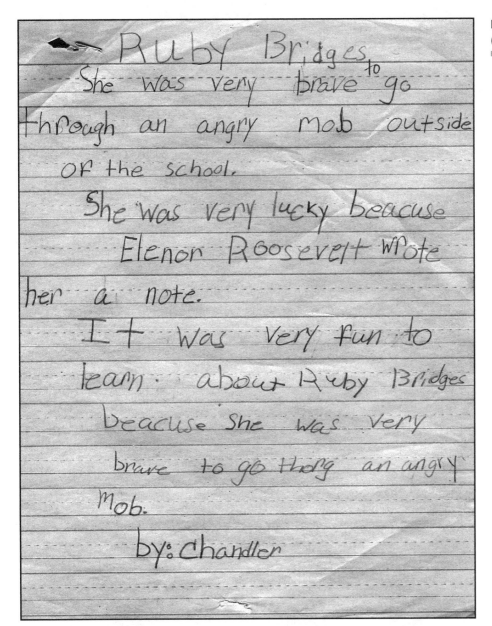

Ruby Bridges
She was very brave to go through an angry mob outside of the school.
She was very lucky beacuse Elenor Roosevelt wrote her a note.
It was very fun to learn about Ruby Bridges beacuse she was very brave to go thong an angry mob.
by: Chandler

tion, and ending of the Revolutionary War; to know the names of major historical figures; to understand the impact the war had on the creation of the United States; and finally to understand the war from a variety of perspectives.

Overview of the Unit

This unit is a preplanned curricular unit based on state and district standards. In fifth grade the major focus for the social studies curriculum is American history. This Revolutionary War unit follows the structure of most units, where the reading and writing workshop are used together to expand students' understanding of historical events. In this unit all students are engaged in the study of the same events; it is a whole-class study and then multigenre writing becomes the culminating activity to allow for student choice, voice, and expression of views on the war.

FIGURE 5.9
Sally's Letter

This is a letter from Sally. She is a little girl standing outside Ruby's school. Her parents are protesting. She wants to go back to school with Ruby.

September 28, 1960

Dear Ruby,

How are you doing in school? Would you it Be scaery to Be you? Ruby I think No other girl would say this but I want to go back to school with you. I Disagree with my parents. parents Don't

Want kids to go School Just becuse of your Skin colro. It's realy boring at home. I wolud Love to Be With you and miss. Henrry. plus I don't have a Broter or Sister. When I Stand Here in the Crod With my parints I Here this word going thro my Head "Ruby we hate you

Exposure and Exploration

For this unit there was a great concern with how children, slaves, patriots, loyalists, and King George viewed the war. So as Suzette's and Ali's classes learned about the war, the teachers made sure to include a variety of perspectives on similar events. They created a class time line to record different events and battles as learned by either the whole class or individuals. The focus began with the events that led up to the war and a study of the major historical people involved. Through the use of read-alouds, guided and shared reading and writing, literature study groups, and investigative groups, children gained a broad understanding of the war.

FIGURE 5.9
(continued)

Ruby We hate"
you those Words going
thore my Head over
and oever aigian.
Wathing you Walk thore
the Door over and over
aigan I am eger to yell
"Whats that's wrong With
you people? She is an EXcelINent
girl!" Ruby Who Kares about
yor skin color? I just
Kare adout us being
firends. Mabey the protesting
Will stop and we can
be friends and go Back to
Schoo to getter.

Love: Sally

Read-Alouds

The unit began with a series of read-alouds on the Revolutionary War (see Appendix B for a list of children's literature used). The teachers used read-alouds to engage students in whole-class discussions of events and stories of the war. They read aloud picture books of historical fiction as well as informational texts and then made them available for students to read again. It was important to explore a variety of genres so children could understand what each genre brought to the topic. They completed an impressions, connections, and wonderings chart (see Chapter 3) for every book read and posted them around the room for reference to their developing understandings of a variety of perspectives on the war. Students also read other books in small groups and completed their own ICW charts.

Each student also kept a literature response log, where they recorded their personal reactions to the books read as a whole group, in pairs, or independently. The structure for these entries was the same as the ICW chart completed as a whole class. In their writer's notebook students recorded their thoughts on the Revolutionary War.

FIGURE 5.10
Ruby's Journal Entry

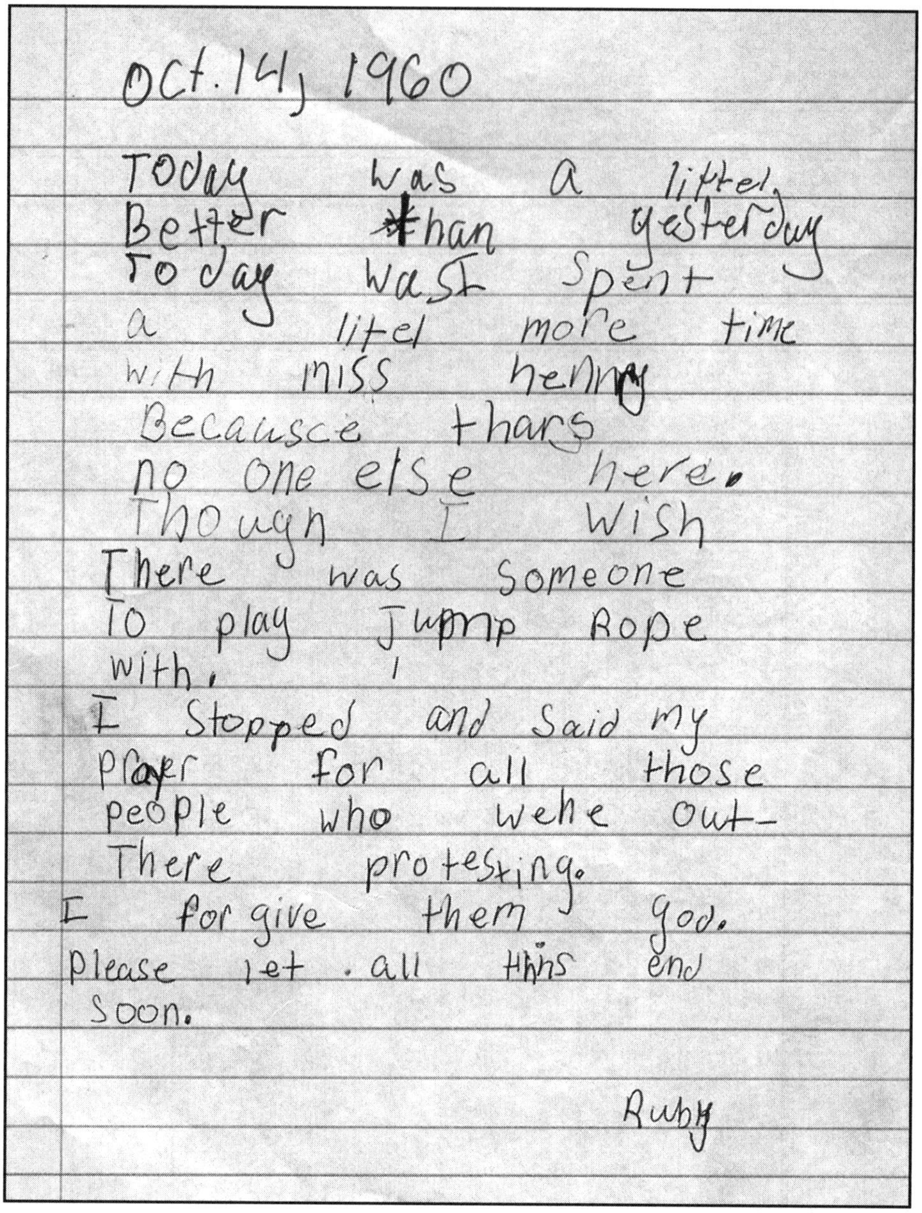

Oct. 14, 1960

Today was a littel
Better than yesterday
To day waS spent
a litel more time
with miss henny
Becausce thars
no one else here.
Though I wish
There was someone
To play Jumnp Rope
with.
I stopped and said my
Prayer for all those
people who wehe out-
There protesting.
I for give them god.
Please let all this end
soon.

Ruby

These entries would later be seeds of writing for their multigenre writing project. For an example, see Figure 5.11, which displays Michaun's journal entry.

Shared and Guided Reading and Writing

The reading for a unit like this can be difficult for many readers. To support their efforts in understanding, students read expository texts in guided reading groups and as a whole class and conducted shared reading of primary sources such as the Declaration of Independence and the Constitution. During an intensive study of these historic documents, writers get a sense of the language and structure of the documents so they may emulate this style in their own writing. In this investigation the teachers conducted a shared (slow) reading of the Declaration of Independence. Students struggled with vocabulary and sentence length and structure. This style was very different from anything they had experienced before. Once students had a good

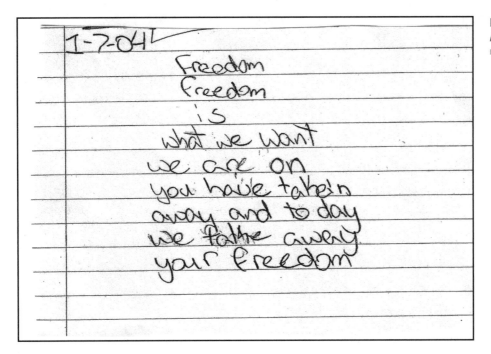

FIGURE 5.11
Michaun's Journal Entry

understanding of the Declaration of Independence the teachers placed them into groups of four and gave each group a section of it to rewrite in their own words. The classes then put it together, dipped it in tea, and hung it in the room for future reading and reference.

Literature Study Groups

To be sure students were exposed to a wide variety of genres, Suzette and Ali formed literature study groups based on the children's area of interest and the books they were interested in reading. Students joined one of seven groups to read historical fiction novels based on the Revolutionary War time period. Those readers who struggled more with the text were supported in one of the following ways: paired reading, a book on CD, or teacher or parent read-aloud at home. All children regardless of reading ability were involved with a book of their choice and were expected to discuss personal responses, the text, the genre, and their understanding of the Revolutionary War in a literature discussion group.

The reading and writing workshops were utilized for whole-class, small-group, and individual investigation. Students read and wrote to enhance their understanding of the Revolutionary War. All the literacy events that led to their eventual multigenre writing projects were important because these events were the foundation for the multigenre writing project. Students were exposed to a variety of genres: poetry, historical fiction, letters, journal entries, primary source documents, expository texts, informational texts, and an array of textbooks. During class discussions students analyzed the variety of genres and how each added to their understanding of this historical time.

Focus on Perspectives

During this unit a major focus was to learn about the war from a variety of perspectives so children would have an understanding of history from different viewpoints.

Ultimately these multiple lenses on history would lend themselves to the writers so they would have a variety of perspectives to choose from when doing their multigenre writing projects.

To transition into multigenre writing, Suzette began with another read-aloud of *Crossing the Delaware: History in Many Voices* (Peacock 1998). This is an interesting picture book telling the events of Washington's crossing of the Delaware. Peacock used three distinctive genres to tell the story—letters, expository and narrative writing, and actual journal entries from officers in the war. Peacock used letter writing to illustrate what a soldier and his girlfriend might converse about and to provide details of events and personal feelings about the war. She also used excerpts from journal entries created by officers in the war and threaded the piece together using a narrative description of the events after a modern-day visit to the House of Decisions as she imagined and recounted what happened there. The use of the three genres is compelling as it provides a layered effect on the reader's understanding of the events surrounding the historic crossing of the Delaware.

Choosing a Focus

Students needed to choose a focus. Even though the focus was much narrower than the research approach, the possibilities were still very broad under the topic of the Revolutionary War. Students needed to decide whether they were going to focus on a historic person, battle, event, or group of people. Students spent two days reviewing the past weeks of classroom research and activities to decide on an interesting focus for their project. The following is a list of possibilities for students to use as their focus:

Paul Revere	George Washington	King George
Martha Washington	patriot child	Loyalist child
Paul Revere's Midnight Ride	slave	Thomas Jefferson
Thomas Jefferson's horse	gun maker	a Hessian soldier
fictitious soldier	Battle of Bunker Hill	Battle of Yorktown
Mrs. Revere	Crossing the Delaware	John Hancock
Revolutionary researcher	Monopoly game board maker	Redcoat soldier

Choosing Perspectives

Once students chose their focus they decided what their perspective was going to be. Students could write from one perspective (e.g., George Washington—all the pieces would be written by George Washington), or they could choose to write from a variety of perspectives (e.g., letters to George from Martha, journal entries by George, letters sent by messenger to the battlefield, correspondence from an English leader demanding a surrender, etc.). Through the experimentation with perspectives, students' choices expanded, as did their understanding of the war. Figure 5.12 displays Will's thinking about the perspective he would use in his letter. Following his decision-making process is his letter from George Washington (see Figure 5.13).

In order to write the letter, Will needed to understand both the details of the Battle of Lexington and Molly Pitcher's involvement, as well as the tone of the letter that George might have written in.

FIGURE 5.12
Will's Thinking

I am doing a death letter from the perspective of George Washington to a family named the James Family. I am writing this because I am studying about the Revolutionary War and in wars people die.

FIGURE 5.13
Will's Letter from George Washington

Dear Mr. and Mrs. James,

Your son Archie James has been shot in the Battle of Lexington. When the British shot most of our men went and burned down the city of Lexington. I took the time to write this letter because he was like a son to me. He was one of my strongest and most favorite men in the army. When he was shot Molly Pitcher saw him and gasped, "Oh, No!" When she saw that there was nobody around she picked him up on her shoulder and yelled, "Help, Someone Help," and no one responded. After there was no response she ran for safety with him on her shoulder. When they were out of danger she set him down and went to get help. Unfortunately Molly and her help returned too late and your son did not make it. I am very sorry.

Sincerely,

George Washington

As students worked through making these writerly decisions, they were ready to complete their multigenre writing proposal; students decided their focus, perspective, audience, reason for the genre to exist, and purpose for each writing piece. Because of the time period, the genres students wrote in were limited. Many students used letters, journals, newspaper articles, epitaphs, poetry, and battle plans, as they were authentic genres of the time.

Ali gave her students an opportunity to inquire about a genre they were unfamiliar with to expand their understanding. She created a form for them to fill out that asked them to identify the genre they wanted to learn more about, the perspective, and the audience and then asked students to record what information they already knew about the topic and books used to locate that information. See Figure 5.14 for Berto's use of this form as he explored a protest sign.

Once students decided their perspective, some investigative groups were formed to help students make decisions about genre or to help them develop the content of their writing pieces.

Investigative Groups

As students chose their focus and perspective, they used investigative groups to discuss and understand the variety of perspectives and opinions about the war. Students were very detailed in their content as they referred to historic places and dates. We will describe just one investigative group because the groups formed during the balloon speech project apply to this investigation as well.

Position on the War

The very nature of the Revolutionary War created a variety of positions and perspectives about the conflict. Therefore two investigative groups were formed to explore the opinions people had about the war and the genres they used and might have used to express these feelings. First, students were grouped by the opposing or differing viewpoints their topic or person of focus had on the war. For example, one

FIGURE 5.14
Berto's Exploration of a Protest Sign

Name Berto

Writing piece I want to get a better background for

Protest Poster _____ (genre)

Perspective Sons of liberty _____

Audience King G. III and to all the loyalists.

What information I can use

All the rude stuff the british
did to the patriots like taking there food
and like takingover there houses
and taxing them and how
they took every body that they fond
prisiners for nothing that they even
did just because they wanted to.

Books I used to find this info
Red coats and Petticoats _____

_____

_____

_____

group consisted of King George, a patriot child, a slave, a black soldier, a patriot soldier, and the Battle of Lexington (see Figure 5.15 for the discussion guide sheet on two of these perspectives).

In this group students filled out the top portion before coming to the group. Then students were prepared to discuss the opinions their perspective or person would have about the war, possible genres used to express these ideas, and then decisions for their own multigenre writing piece. Second, students were grouped by similar perspectives on the war and again discussed the opinions and variety of genres that were available to them.

During these groups students expanded their understanding of the Revolutionary War, genres used during that time, and genre possibilities for their writing. This genre lens on historic events afforded children a very different conversation about the war as they discussed *how* people were able to record events, correspond with each other, and communicate directions and opinions effectively.

Opposing viewpoints of the Revolutionary War
Discussion Guide

Focus: *slave*   *patriot child*

Opinions of war:

cofused   loyal to parents
· hypcritical   scaed of war
· hopeful for their own   sad for others
freedom   children who must leave

Genres used to express these opinions:

song   journals
prayer   games
stories   books
                             prayers

Genres I might like to try:

journals   journal   letters
poetry   story   poetry
story   news artikl
Obichucary   jump rope rhime

Drafting Multigenre Projects

As students completed their writing proposals, they began to draft their writing pieces utilizing all the multigenre activities listed previously. They explored genres; critically read; defined and experimented with genres; conducted peer conferences; and revised, edited, and published the projects.

We now share samples from one completed project. Figure 5.16 displays a few parts of Jamie's project. He chose to focus on a fictitious soldier he named Mike Snag. His pieces included battle plans he received from George Washington, a death letter to Mike Snag's family, and the obituary as it appeared in the newspaper. When exploring this project, it was evident that Jamie was thoughtful about the content, appropriate genres, and his project's visual appearance.

FIGURE 5.16
Jamie's Project

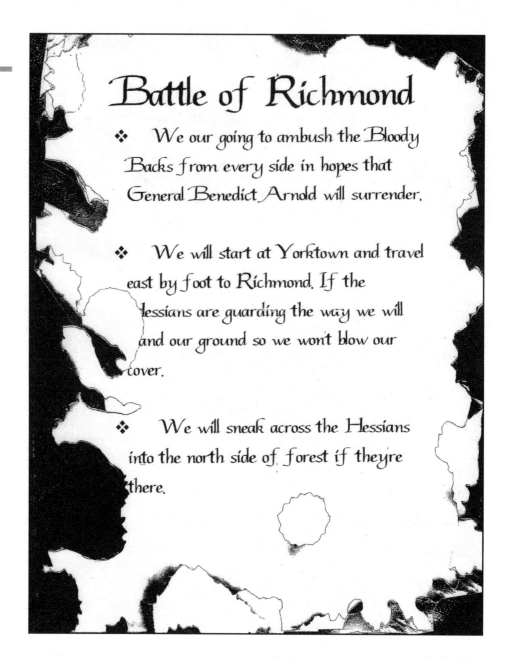

Battle of Richmond

❖ We our going to ambush the Bloody Backs from every side in hopes that General Benedict Arnold will surrender.

❖ We will start at Yorktown and travel east by foot to Richmond. If the Hessians are guarding the way we will and our ground so we won't blow our cover.

❖ We will sneak across the Hessians into the north side of forest if they're there.

The projects we've described in this chapter are alternatives to the traditional multigenre writing project and might be a way to experiment with multigenre writing as an extension of curricular items. Multigenre writing could be utilized in the science content areas as well, expanding on or replacing the science report. However teachers and students enter into multigenre writing, a deep understanding of the topic is the foundation and the multiple genres allow students to obtain a layered understanding. In the last section we offer yet one more way to express understanding through multiple genres.

FIGURE 5.16
(continued)

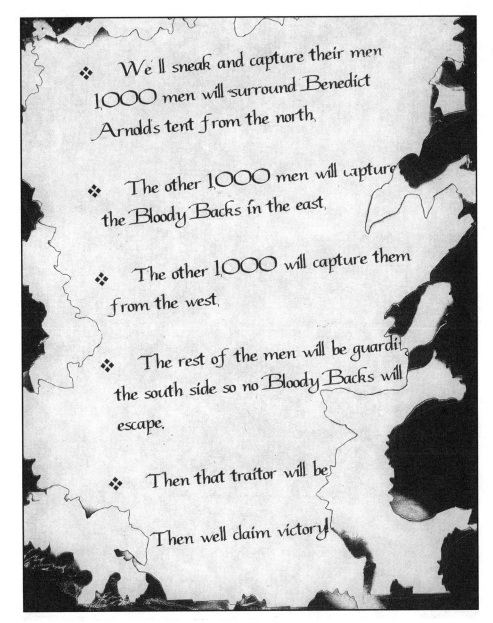

❖ We'll sneak and capture their men 1,000 men will surround Benedict Arnold's tent from the north,

❖ The other 1,000 men will capture the Bloody Backs in the east,

❖ The other 1,000 will capture them from the west,

❖ The rest of the men will be guarding the south side so no Bloody Backs will escape.

❖ Then that traitor will be

Then we'll claim victory!

Multigenre Writing as a Response to Literature

Our last alternative for multigenre writing is as a response to literature. When children use multigenre writing as a response to literature, they are entering into the story world of the characters and interpreting what characters would say in response to a particular situation, what they might say to another character, or what an outside voice or character not in the book would write or say about them.

This type of response is certainly not a replacement for quality discussions or other types of response, but it requires children to have a deep understanding of the literature because interpretation is necessary as they create writing pieces from a variety of perspectives. In this section we describe how children of various ages used particular reading strategies to understand a book in depth before beginning their

FIGURE 5.16
(continued)

multigenre writing project and then how students engaged in multigenre writing as a response to literature.

Voices in the Park

For this particular unit of study Suzette read *Voices in the Park* (Browne 2001) in a series of read-alouds and discussion activities to a multiage class of first, second, and third graders. This was a week-and-a-half unit of study on this particular book. Students had read other Anthony Browne books and as a class wanted to further investigate this book. *Voices in the Park* is a complex picture book that tells about an outing of four people, a mother and her son and a father and his daughter. The book is told in separate voices and in first person as each character tells about his or her simultaneous experience in the park one day. This is a story of friendship, class, and point of view as Browne allows the

FIGURE 5.16
(continued)

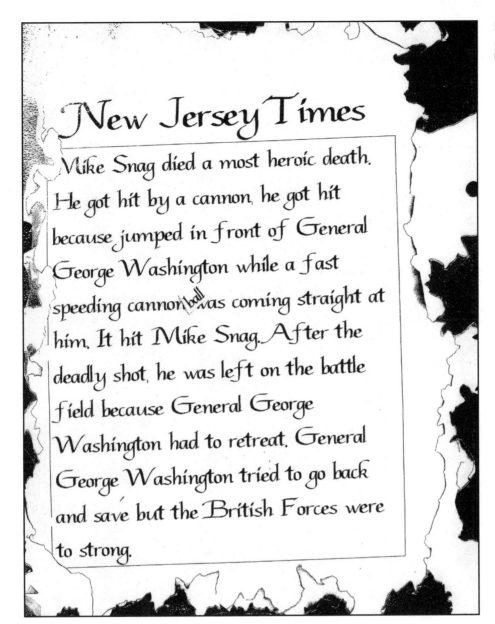

New Jersey Times

Mike Snag died a most heroic death. He got hit by a cannon, he got hit because jumped in front of General George Washington while a fast speeding cannonball was coming straight at him. It hit Mike Snag. After the deadly shot, he was left on the battle field because General George Washington had to retreat. General George Washington tried to go back and save but the British Forces were to strong.

reader to enter into the characters' world and understand life from each perspective. The text of this book is simple but the story is extended through the illustrations, which require time for readers to notice and interpret the visual elements.

In order for children to engage in multigenre writing as a response, they first need a deep understanding of the text, for they cannot articulate their interpretations if they do not understand it. *Voices in the Park* is complex as the voices are separate and tell the story that occurred at the exact same moment, so children need time to ponder and to understand the interplay between text and illustrations.

Suzette began this unit with a read-aloud of *Voices in the Park*. After the read-aloud she and the students completed an impressions, connections, and wonderings chart. Students shared their ideas and initial thoughts about the picture book. Following is an example of the students' responses to the book.

FIGURE 5.16
(continued)

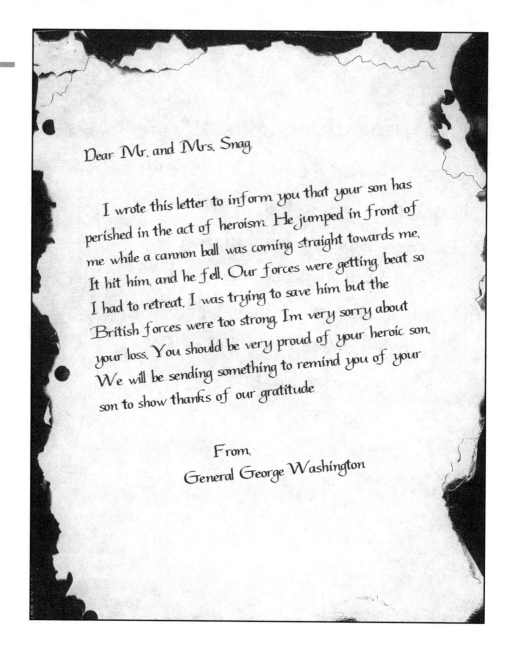

Dear Mr. and Mrs. Snag,

I wrote this letter to inform you that your son has perished in the act of heroism. He jumped in front of me while a cannon ball was coming straight towards me. It hit him, and he fell. Our forces were getting beat so I had to retreat. I was trying to save him but the British forces were too strong. I'm very sorry about your loss. You should be very proud of your heroic son. We will be sending something to remind you of your son to show thanks of our gratitude

From,
General George Washington

Impressions

❖ Charles is sad.

❖ The trees represent that he wants to climb the tree but his mother is going to get mad.

❖ The lampposts are shaped like the mom's hat and there are white clouds in them.

❖ On Charles' side of the park the trees are dead and on Smudge's side it is all light because Charles is amazed and Smudge is happy.

Connections

❖ He uses the color red to show power like in his other books, especially *Gorilla* (Browne 1983) and *Willy the Wimp* (Browne 1995).

- The parents are sad and busy like in *Gorilla*.
- There is a problem with Charles like the mom in *The Piggybook* (1986).

Wonderings

- Why did the mom take Charles to the park if he can't play?
- What does the fruit represent in Smudge's story?
- Why is the text so simple?
- Why is the mom so mean and why does she think the dad is a "frightful type"?

The second day Suzette read the book again and brought in multiple copies of *Voices in the Park* for children to follow along with and to reread after the read-aloud. After the second read-aloud the class added to their impressions, connections, and wonderings chart.

Suzette then completed a disruption-of-text activity (Serafini 2006). In this activity the illustrations and the text are separated and children spend time attending to each in isolation; then they come back together and discuss the impact the parts have on the whole. First Suzette divided the class into four groups, and two looked at the illustrations and two looked at the text. Suzette made two complete color copies of the illustrations without the text and displayed the illustrations on two separate walls in a storyboard fashion. For thirty minutes students in two small groups studied and discussed what they noticed and what meaning they could apply to only the illustrations. They recorded their ideas on a worksheet that was divided into four sections: first ideas, text only, illustrations only, and new interpretations about the book. On this form students recorded their ideas about the book from the first two read-alouds and then recorded ideas during their small-group investigations.

The other two groups received a typed copy of the text from *Voices in the Park* and did a readers' theatre reading of the text. After the reading they discussed and recorded the interpretations they had by attending to the text only. Because the illustrations are so compelling in this book, students needed time to attend to the text and how the words and structure enhance and at times contradict the story told through the illustrations. The next day the students switched groups and completed the process again. On the last day each group received a copy of the book; they read it again and shared new insights they had based on the disruption-of-text activity.

This in-depth study of a picture book is necessary to help children understand the characters, setting, themes, and symbols throughout the book. In these small discussion groups, students listen to their classmates and expand their understanding as new possibilities for meaning are presented. This activity allows children to understand the book at a deeper level as they investigate the interplay between text and illustrations.

Once the discussion and investigation of *Voices in the Park* was completed, the class then brainstormed genres that would be appropriate for the characters in the book. Suzette and the children discussed what kind of writing these characters might do and what someone else might write about or to them. The following is a list of possible genres and topics the students shared:

❖ job application for the dad

❖ birthday invitation from Smudge to Charles

❖ journal entries from Charles, or any character

❖ to-do list for the maids while Mother and Charles are at the park

❖ letters or journal entries from the dogs' point of view

❖ letters to the characters from Anthony Browne

❖ map of the park

❖ relaxation flyer for Mother to visit a spa

❖ job wanted flyer

❖ labels for Charles' playthings

❖ drawing of Smudge's room

❖ thank-you letter for the flower from Smudge

❖ journal entry from sad and happy Santa Claus

The brainstorming session was as powerful as the actual writing as students shared ideas on character development and character motivation. As they decided on a genre, they explained why the character might write something like that, and their choice of audience demonstrated their understanding of the interconnectedness of each character.

During the writing time, Suzette spent her time conferencing with students and discussing their reasoning for their genre choices. She asked:

❖ Who is writing the piece?

❖ Who is the audience?

❖ Why would he or she write it?

At this level it was important for the children to articulate verbally rather than have them struggle through writing a defense. In this manner children were able to focus on the content of their piece. Each child was able to answer these questions and understood why the piece was appropriate for the character. Figure 5.17 provides an example of third grader Mathew's letter to a paint company written from the father's point of view, asking for a job, and a response from the paint company. In this example, Mathew understood the plight of the father and his desperation as a single father to take care of his daughter.

Through the multigenre writing project, students explored the feelings of each character and were required to interpret the character's personality as well as intentions through their choice of genre. At the end of the project students shared their writing pieces with the class and explained their choice of genre and why the character might have written it. The following are some of the ideas they shared about their genre choices:

FIGURE 5.17
Matthew's Letter and Response

> Dear paint company
> I hope you under-
> stand. I am a single
> father. So if you give
> me a job I might have
> to miss days but I will call
> and tell if I will miss
> a day. I will work hard.

> Dear John you've got
> the job come to
> work on fraiday 9:00.
> I'm glad you got
> the job. I hope you
> get enough money
> to feed you and you'r
> daughter.

❖ The father would have written a letter to a paint company asking for a job. He probably would have just gone there but the letter shows what he might have said. I think he would do whatever it takes to get a job. He had hope.

❖ I think that the dogs were very friendly and did not think the same way as their owners; they did not care about money or clothes or what kind of dog they were, they just played. So I think that if they could they would have written a letter to each other saying thanks for a fun time in the park.

❖ Smudge was happy, Charlie gave her a flower so she would say thanks and I think she would draw a picture for him.

As students shared their projects they expressed even more understanding than what their actual genre could show. Through this sharing students had new interpretations about the book as they thought about what each character might say and how they were each related to each other. They also discussed their personal reactions to the story and shared their thoughts on why Anthony Browne wrote the story.

Multigenre writing provides a different avenue to discuss literature as children share and negotiate their own interpretations about the text, but they also use genre as an avenue for discussion as they interpret the kinds of writing or speaking the character might do outside of the story. In order for this discussion and writing project to be effective, students must have an in-depth understanding of the text, themes, and tone of the story.

Unit on Building Community

In this last example, the multigenre writing was in response to a selection of books all pertaining to the theme of building community. For this unit we draw from Ali and Lisa's sixth-grade classroom. Ali and Lisa conducted a unit of study described in Serafini and Serafini Young's book *Around the Reading Workshop in 180 Days* (2006).

To begin the school year Ali and Lisa read many picture books (see Appendix C for a list of these books) that all have a similar theme of accepting differences and living together differently. The first book they read was *The Straight Line Wonder* (Fox 1997). In this story a straight line no longer wishes to remain straight; he wants to jump in humps and twirl in whirls. His friends tell him to stay straight or people will stare. At the end of the book a movie director discovers the straight line and makes him a star and the other lines accept him for who he is.

After reading the book aloud students engaged in a discussion about it and also how the ideas presented in the book might apply to their classroom community. Ali and Lisa completed an ICW chart. Following are some student responses to *The Straight Line Wonder.*

Impressions

❖ The straight sine is a strong character.

❖ I think the straight line is not like a real kid; it is too tough to be exactly who you want to be—people laugh when you try.

Connections

❖ This book reminds me of Molly Lou Melon and how she was not afraid to be herself.

❖ In Horace and Morris, the struggle to be the kind of girl and boy they want to be but in the end they compromise; the straight line did not give in to his friends—they all changed instead.

❖ This reminds me of when I was teased for being short.

❖ It reminds me of how I go along with everything my friends want to do.

Wonderings

❖ Why did the friends only like him when he became famous?

❖ How did the straight line become so strong?

❖ Was Mem Fox strong like him?

❖ Did she know someone like that?

❖ What would happen if we twirled in whirls?

Each day Ali and Lisa read a different book that built on the discussions they'd had about community the previous day. During the writing workshop time, Ali and Lisa began a discussion about genre and created a list of the genres they were familiar with. As they were creating this list, they also discussed ways to respond to literature. They introduced the literature response log that students would be required to respond in, but they also introduced multigenre writing as a response to literature.

They discussed that as the students became familiar with characters and themes of books, they could choose a variety of genres and perspectives to write from.

At the end of the week Ali and Lisa asked students to choose a book and then to choose a multigenre writing project they would like to complete in response to that particular book. They gave students the following guidelines:

- ❖ Choose a text.
- ❖ Determine the important things you got from the text.
- ❖ Determine what genre would be the most appropriate for your response or, rather, which one fits best.
- ❖ Write your response and remember to show understanding.

Before students began their own projects, Ali and Lisa modeled one for them. They chose *Stand Tall Molly Lou Melon* (Lovell 2001). In this book a very small girl with a squeaky voice and buckteeth lives with her grandmother, who teaches her to stand tall and to be proud of herself. When Molly Lou Melon moves to a new school, she encounters a bully who puts her grandmother's lessons to the test. In the end standing tall wins out and wins the respect of the school bully. Here is the letter the teachers typed in front of their students and projected for all to see.

> Dear Molly Lou Melon,
> I think you are an extremely unique, strong and brave person. I really like the way you are different and not afraid to be yourself. I really admire the positive way you handled the situation with that bully, Ronald.
> I'm reading another book about a girl named Stargirl, who reminds me of you in the way that she's not afraid to be different. Like you, Stargirl is unique and proud of her talents. Thank you for inspiring me to be strong and unique.
>
> Sincerely,
> Miss Gamble

As a class they discussed their choice of book and choice of genre. Ali and Lisa shared how the letter genre would be a great choice to share personal feelings about Molly Lou Melon and to share directly with the character the connections to other literature they were making in reference to her story. Other genre possibilities were letters to Ronald, a no-bullying poster, letters to Grandma, journal entries, a list of sayings from Grandma to remember, and a book on how to be yourself and to stand up to bullies.

Ali and Lisa then invited students to create their own multigenre writing projects. Many students completed numerous responses to a variety of characters and books. Figures 5.18 and 5.19 present two student examples. These examples demonstrate students' ability to connect with characters and to understand the overall themes of the unit as well as to interpret characters' feelings and how other characters might relate to them. In order for students to engage in this kind of response they must have a deep understanding of the story, characters, and author's intentions and have a deep personal connection with the story and the message.

Multigenre writing is a powerful and exciting avenue for children to choose as they experiment with audiences and perspectives and discover multiple purposes

FIGURE 5.18
Response to Straight Line Wonder

Strait line
Wonder
(Diary)

Dear Diary,   7/15/06
   Today I decided not to be strait any more.
So I started jumping in humps. My friends
told me to stop because people would
stare. Oh, don't worry. I told them I didn't
mind. They don't understand that I have
to be myself some times.   7/16/06

Dear Diary,
   Today. I now started to twirl in whirls!
My friends are still with me, but they're
a little mad, but, I don't care, at least they
are still with me. Anyway. twirling in whirls
was fun.   7/17/06

Dear Diary,
   Now today, I started pointing my joints,
creeped in heeps, and springed my rings. But
now my friends ditched me for being me. I'm
a little depressed, but I'm not ever going to
be strait. Not again!   7/18/06

Dear Diary,
Today I went to a whole new level! I jumped
in humps, twirled in whirls, pointed my joints,
creeped in heeps and springed in rings all at
the same time!   7/19/06

Dear Diary, today while I was doing my wild
stunts, a famous movie director found me and
I starred in his new MOVIE!

while choosing a variety of genres to express their expanding understanding of topic and genre. Multigenre writing can be used as a unit all by itself, as an exploration and representation of research, or as an extension of a unit of study that already exists in the curriculum. Through this kind of writing, students make many more decisions about their writing and have many more choices to enter into writing in comparison to prompt writing, which affords students little choice or voice. This chapter outlines a variety of ways to enter into this kind of writing and it is only a small example of the ways multigenre writing can be used for explorations and expression.

FIGURE 5.19
Response to The Piggybook

It is important to note that not all of these multigenre writing projects occur within one academic year. Suzette conducted the balloon speeches each year while teaching in Colorado and used multigenre as an extension. In separate years and classrooms the Revolutionary War unit was conducted as well as the responses to literature. It is important to look at the existing curriculum and find places where multigenre writing will benefit children and their understanding of topic and genre.

References

Allen, C. A. 2001. *The Multigenre Research Paper: Voice, Passion and Discovery in Grades 4–6.* Portsmouth, NH: Heinemann.

Browne, A. 1983. *Gorilla.* Cambridge, MA: Candlewick Press.

———. 1986. *The Piggybook.* New York: DK.

————. 1995. *Willy the Wimp*. New York: Walker Books.

————. 2001. *Voices in the Park*. New York: DK.

Fox, M. 1997. *The Straight Line Wonder*. New York: Mondo Publishing

Lovell, P. 2001. *Stand Tall Molly Lou Melon*. New York: G. P. Putnam's Sons.

Peacock, L. 1998. *Crossing the Delaware: A History in Many Voices*. New York: Simon and Schuster.

Romano, T. 2000. *Blending Genre, Altering Style: Writing Multigenre Papers*. Portsmouth, NH: Boynton/Cook.

Sendak, M. 1963. *Where the Wild Things Are*. New York: Harper and Row.

Serafini, F. 2001. *The Reading Workshop: Creating Space for Readers*. Portsmouth, NH: Heinemann.

Serafini, F., and S. Serafini Youngs. 2006. *Around the Reading Workshop in 180 Days*. Portsmouth, NH: Heinemann.

CHAPTER 6

Assessing the Multigenre Process and Project

SUZETTE: So what can you share with teachers about multigenre writing?

NANCY: Students need time to come up with ideas, they need time to brainstorm, conference with each other, think of what they're going to do and does it work. They need time to draft, they need time to revise and edit each piece. And I don't have a problem with the time as long as they are on task and learning . . . but it does take a long time.

SUZETTE: Anything else?

NANCY: Just lots of examples, lots of discussion, and then lots of little conferences about how each piece fits. Multigenre projects moved them from just looking at each writing piece as a separate event. They needed to see how each piece supported the other. I had to learn to help them with this.

SUZETTE: How did you assess what they did?

NANCY: I just looked at the whole project: some of them were really strong at certain things and some were weaker in other areas. Just like with other writing, I considered their revisions, editing, the illustrations, and how the project worked together. I found some kids were stuck on pictures and couldn't take their thinking into writing. Other kids were vice versa; they had all the writing but couldn't think of visual things to put in their books. I had a rubric and we used that for the final evaluation. The kids knew what was expected.

Nancy and Suzette engaged in a retrospective conversation about multigenre writing at the end of a school year. Nancy articulated what was new for her students in multigenre writing—using multiple pieces to create a whole, more complex project. She highlighted the time it takes to support students through such a process. Finally, she talked a bit about how she assessed her students' writing. In this conversation about assessment she noted that it is both the process and the final product that she assesses as each reveals a different facet of a student's knowledge.

Nancy is not unlike other teachers in that she recognizes that the time for multigenre projects is time not spent in other writing, and therefore, it must have value to students' growth as writers and readers for her to carve out the time within her curriculum (Barone and Taylor 2006). Currently, teachers feel pressure on their curriculum as students are assessed in reading, writing, math, and other subjects to determine their school's proficiency in student achievement (Afflerbach 2005). Additionally, with the advent of the National Reading Panel report (2000), reading instruction and learning moved to the forefront of research and instruction while writing instruction and learning receded. Because of the increased attention to reading, teachers often find it more difficult to allow for writing workshop time in their classrooms, thus making this time even more precious than it once might have been.

Moreover, teachers are conflicted in preparing for tests and meeting the expectations of their curriculum (Calkins et al. 1998; Shelton and Fu 2004). Teachers like Nancy take a critical view of multigenre projects to determine if they support students in important literacy skills and knowledge as expected in school, district, state, and national standards. Throughout this chapter, we provide evidence to support the use of multigenre writing for meeting a myriad of student learning expectations.

Our view of assessment as documented through multigenre writing is grounded in eight principles of classroom-based literacy assessment (Cooper 1997):

1. Assessment must be an ongoing process. Students are assessed as they participate in multiple literacy activities throughout each academic year.

2. Assessment is an integral part of instruction. It allows a teacher to determine how a student is doing and to compare students within a class. It provides an opportunity for teachers to revise instructional plans.

3. Assessment is best when it is authentic. Teachers get the best information about student reading and writing achievement when students engage in reading and writing activities, rather than in testing experiences.

4. Assessment is a collaborative, reflective process. When students collaborate with other students or the teacher, they reflect on what they have learned and how they can improve.

5. Assessment is best when it is multidimensional. Teachers learn more about students when they have students engage in a variety of literacy activities.

6. Assessment should be developmentally and culturally appropriate. Assessment tasks that have single right answers limit the ability of students to demonstrate partially constructed knowledge.

7. Assessment is expected to identify student strengths. Children learn best when they move from what they know to new strategies or skills.

8. Assessments must be developed around the current scientific base of how students learn to read and write.

Importantly, multigenre writing is evidenced in each of these principles and thus is appropriate for ongoing classroom assessment. For instance, multigenre writing is an ongoing process, is authentic, is collaborative, and allows students to move from their strengths. Teachers can therefore use these data to group students and to determine the most effective instruction to help students achieve.

In this chapter, we consider both formal assessments (including those used to determine annual yearly progress [AYP]) and classroom-based assessments that result in carefully constructed student learning experiences. Additionally, we visit local and national standards and address how multigenre projects support these learning expectations. Throughout this chapter we use student projects to enrich this discussion of assessment.

National, State, and Local Assessments

The National Assessment of Educational Progress (NAEP) is considered to be the nation's report card (see nces.ed.gov/nationsreportcard). Over the past thirty-five years, NAEP has provided an independent measure of what students across the United States know and can do in reading, mathematics, science, and writing as well as other core subject areas. NAEP has been reporting state-by-state results since 1990. The NAEP writing assessment presents a broad view of how well America's students are writing. The assessment prompts are focused on the following three purposes for writing to ensure that they reflect writing genres receiving the most emphasis in classroom instruction:

❖ Narrative writing (telling a story)—writers incorporate their imagination and creativity in the production of stories or personal essays;

❖ Informative writing (informing the reader)—writers provide the reader with information, e.g., reporting on events or analyzing concepts; and

❖ Persuasive writing (persuading the reader)—writers seek to persuade the reader to take action or to bring about change.

NAEP provides findings for writing assessments from 1998 to 2002, when the last assessment occurred. Students' average scores on the NAEP writing assessment increased between 1998 and 2002 at grades 4 and 8. However, no significant change was detected in the performance of twelfth graders between the two assessment years. NAEP then disaggregates the results so that states and schools have a sense of which students are doing well and where. For instance:

❖ Fourth-grade writing scores at the 10th to the 90th percentiles increased between 1998 and 2002. This means that the performance of high-, middle-, and low-performing students improved between the two years.

❖ The average scores of male and female fourth and eighth graders were higher in 2002 than in 1998.

❖ At grades 4 and 8, white, black, and Hispanic students had higher average writing scores in 2002 than in 1998.

❖ Average fourth- and eighth-grade writing scores in 2002 were higher than in 1998 for students who were eligible for free or reduced-price lunch, as well as for those who were not eligible.

When considering the expectations of this assessment, it is clear that NAEP is evaluating students' writing of a variety of genres. Students are expected to understand the genre so well that they can craft a powerful piece of writing. When comparing these expectations to the instructional and learning implications of multigenre writing, the parallels are transparent. As teachers engage students in multigenre writing, they prepare them for real writing tasks and in addition for the expectations of the NAEP writing assessment.

States refer to this data and use it to determine how their students are doing in writing in comparison with students in other states; however, they also rely on state writing assessments to determine how students are performing in writing in their state. Each state chooses at which academic grades to assess student writing (most often fourth or fifth grade), and all states expect students to perform in multiple ways. Some states combine a writing assignment with a multiple-choice test that targets details such as grammar. Other states rely on a single writing performance to determine writing achievement. By visiting the website http://accountability.ccsso.org, educators can learn about the assessments required in each state. Typically state writing assessments match the expectations documented in state standards. More discussion of state standards occurs in the next section.

State writing assessments are very visible as they contribute to a school's annual performance and help determine whether it has achieved AYP status. In most states these results appear on the state department of education's website and on each school district's website. Districts can see which schools are meeting the demands of the writing assessment and where there are needs. Each school receives a report comparing its district with the state averages. In addition, each school receives a report comparing it with the district averages and it receives individual reports for each student.

Most states expect students to write to a prompt, such as *Explain a time when you felt important.* Students have time to brainstorm, write a first draft, and revise and edit. Often the writing test takes more than a single day. States usually evaluate each writing assessment using writing traits. For instance, each student gets a score of 1 (not proficient) to 4 (proficient) on each trait. These results target areas where students have strengths or difficulties such as ideas, organization, voice, and conventions.

The question pertinent to multigenre writing for teachers is Does this writing prepare students to do well on these assessments? The assessments expect students to use all of the traits to compose either a narrative, informational, or persuasive piece of writing. We believe that this is exactly what multigenre does. It allows students to explore multiple genres and combine them in powerful ways. Through this process, students learn to select the most appropriate genre, write it to a particular audience, and in many cases build a persuasive argument about its use. Students argue for their choices in the defenses and can articulate their preferred choice. This writing prepares them for the challenges of an on-the-spot writing assessment in authentic ways that also build their knowledge of the writing craft.

Although the state writing test is the most visible writing assessment for states and schools, some districts and schools also have similar writing assessments in place. If the writing assessment is at a district level, it parallels the expectations of the state. At a school level, we have seen the whole school write to a prompt such as *Write about something that you do well.* Students have time for prewriting, drafting, revision, and editing. Teachers then evaluate students' writing to guide instruction for the year. Periodically throughout the year, they ask students to again write to a prompt. They then use these additional writing assessments to determine the progress of their students. These writing assessments are less visible to those outside the school and directly target instruction. Once again, since these formats are so similar to other writing assessments, multigenre writing holds up strong. It prepares students to integrate the traits and write in a rich variety of genres. Students learn how to make the best case for their writing through nuanced changes in genre.

National, State, and Local Standards

The standards movement began in the 1980s. At this time President George H. W. Bush called a meeting of all governors to discuss the disappointing national student achievement data. Following this, the U.S. Congress established the National Council on Education Standards and Testing (NCEST). This group recommended national standards and assessments (Valencia and Wixson 2001). At this point, many national disciplinary groups came together to establish national standards as states and districts worked on their own standards documents.

In literacy, the National Council of Teachers of English and the International Reading Association collaborated on standards for the English language arts (see www.ncte.org/about/over/standards). They identified twelve major standards:

1. Students read a wide range of print and nonprint texts.
2. Students read a wide range of literature from many periods in many genres.
3. Students apply a wide range of strategies to comprehend, interpret, evaluate, and appreciate texts.
4. Students adjust their use of spoken, written, and visual language to communicate effectively.
5. Students employ a wider range of strategies as they write and use different writing process elements.
6. Students apply knowledge of language structure, language conventions, media techniques, figurative language, and genre to create, critique, and discuss print and non-print texts.
7. Students conduct research on issues and interests by generating ideas and questions.
8. Students use a variety of technological and information resources to gather and synthesize information.
9. Students develop an understanding of and respect for diversity in language use, patterns, and dialects across cultures.
10. Students whose first language is not English make use of their first language to develop competency.
11. Students participate as knowledgeable, reflective, creative, and critical members of literacy communities.
12. Students use spoken, written, and visual language to accomplish their own purposes.

Once again the national standards parallel the expectations of multigenre writing. If we move through the standards linearly, the matches are clear. First, students read many print and nonprint texts in crafting their multigenre projects. Second, as has been shown in previous examples, students learn about literature and writing from various historical periods. Third, students use multiple strategies to comprehend text and to create their own and they adjust their language when they create and share their projects. Fourth, students use the writing process and learn to write in a wide range of genres for different audiences. Through this writing they apply and develop their knowledge of language structures and writing conventions. Fifth, students pose questions that guide their projects and they find answers to these questions through multiple data sources. Sixth, students gain respect for others and understand different cultural practices through their research. Seventh, students are part of a literacy community within their classroom and they use spoken, written, and visual language in their projects and through sharing their projects. The only national standard not addressed deals with the issue of which language to use.

Each state also has a standards document. The easiest way to find each state's standards document is through the state department of education's website. At this website, the department details each major standard with subgoals listed below. For instance, in New York, speaking and writing are connected. Students are expected to speak and write for critical analysis and evaluation. The state suggests that evidence of this standard appears when students write a persuasive letter, give an oral report, participate in a group discussion centered on text, write an analysis, and work in a writing group. We found it interesting that writing in a variety of genres is not explicitly mentioned. The focus appears to be on persuasive writing (www.emsc.nysed.gov/). We also explored the writing standards for the fourth grade in California (www.cde.ca.gov/). Unlike New York, California expects fourth-grade students to write narratives, responses to literature, and informational reports. It also has a writing standard that focuses solely on writing conventions.

All state standards address writing within English language arts. Some of the writing standards are not as focused on specific genres, but they all expect students to write clear, well-organized pieces with writing conventions in place. Not surprisingly, multigenre writing, although not targeted as a standard, supports the skills and knowledge about writing addressed in state standards. Additionally, it includes oral presentation and technology, such as the use of PowerPoint, and further addresses other standards. As a result, teachers can feel comfortable that when they encourage students to engage in multigenre projects, they are in fact teaching to their state standards.

Many school districts considered their state standards and created their own standards. Often these standards expect more of students than do the state's standards and are more specific in what students are expected to know. We reviewed the district standards in a local school district. We discovered that for writing, students by the end of fourth grade must be able to: (1) write a narrative; (2) write responses to texts; (3) generate a variety of creative genres such as drama, poetry, or short stories; (4) critically analyze literature; (5) write a summary; and (6) write an informational text with supporting detail. The writing standard also includes subordinating areas targeted to conventions and grammar. Although multigenre projects do not directly include responses to texts, they support the other fourth-grade writing standards for this school district.

What we believe to be important about standards is that teachers are familiar with their state and local district standards so that they can explicitly match up how their multigenre projects target each expected standard. Through this perusal, they can clarify how they are meeting the expected curriculum teaching expectations and how their students are acquiring these skills and processes.

Student Assessment Through Portfolios

In this section, we move from a broad perspective of high-stakes assessment and standards to classroom-based assessment tied to multigenre projects. We use portfolios so that teachers and students can see the process of the multigenre projects as well as the final products.

There are many types of portfolios, which include

- ❖ showcase portfolios, which highlight a student's work

- ❖ documentation portfolios, which keep a record of achievement

- ❖ evaluation portfolios, which are completed by teachers to report achievement

- ❖ process portfolios, which describe the learning journey

- ❖ composite portfolios, which include elements from the other portfolio types (Valencia 1998)

For this chapter, we are viewing the multigenre portfolio as a combination of the showcase, process, and evaluation portfolios. It has elements of a showcase portfolio, as the final multigenre product is included and shared with students, teachers, and parents. Students document their process of completing the multigenre project and often include earlier drafts to show changes they have made, reflecting the process portfolio. Finally, teachers and students evaluate the completed multigenre project, supporting an evaluation portfolio.

Early on in the multigenre process, we talked about organization of all of the writing included in such a project (see Chapters 2 and 3). For the portfolio, a teacher would find a suitable folder for writing. It could be as simple as a folded piece of construction paper. This becomes the portfolio container. Teachers develop their personal structure for collecting work to be placed into the portfolio. For instance, they may decide that on a certain day all lists of genres for a student's project need to be placed into the portfolio. As with the defense, they may ask students to reflect on these choices. In Figure 6.1, Harmony explains why she has included a birth announcement. It is clear in her argument for the birth announcement that it fills a void in the writing about Martin Luther King Jr.

Or teachers may specify writing and/or forms that need to be in the portfolio and allow students more flexibility as to when they place these entries into it. These details need to match the teacher's learning expectations, as there is no best way to organize this process.

To facilitate the evaluation part of a multigenre project, we share several projects from third through sixth graders so that teachers can get a sense of what might be expected from students and how they might respond to student work. The projects reflect a full spectrum of student work from simple to complex. What doesn't show in these completed projects are the thinking, reading, conversing, and reflecting that occurred as they were completed.

FIGURE 6.1
Harmony's Reflection

The peice that I am doing is a birth announcement about Martin Luther King Jr. I'm doing this because I wanted to learn more about Martin Luther King Jr. when he was a baby. Most books about him don't talk about when he was a baby.

by

Harmony

Harmony's Multigenre Portfolio

Harmony's project as a third grader includes three genres: birth announcement, poem, and beginning of a story. She has written three defenses, or reflections on why she selected these genres. Looking at these pieces (see Figures 6.2 through 6.6), we provide a possible teacher evaluation of strengths and then needs of the final product and the writing process.

Multigenre Project—Strengths

1. The student completed three different genres around the topic of Martin Luther King Jr.

2. The pieces support each other in that they share different parts of his life.

3. The project is neat and carefully edited.

4. Harmony clearly understood the genres of a birth announcement and an acrostic poem.

5. The project was turned in on time.

6. Visuals and interesting fonts were used.

7. Harmony made an interesting word choice in using the word *influenced*.

FIGURE 6.2
Harmony's Birth Announcement

Birth Announcement in paper

Mr. and Mrs. Martin King had a little baby boy. His name is Martin Luther King Jr. He was born on January 15, 1929. He weighed 7 pounds 10 ounces and was 20 inch long. The couple are proud to have a healthy, new addition to the family.

FIGURE 6.3
Defense of Poem

I wrote an acrostic poem about Martin Luther King Jr. to show how he influenced our lives.

FIGURE 6.4
Acrostic Poem

Martin
Active
Radio
Teacher
Intelligent
Newspaper

FIGURE 6.5
Story Defense

> I wrote this two page book so it could be a mystery. I want the readers to finish the story.

FIGURE 6.6
Two-Page Story

Mr. and Mrs. King were so happy that they had a new baby. He was so good when he was a baby. Over the years he grew into a young boy.	Martin was very smart and did well in school. He had a lot of friends and everybody liked him.

Multigenre Project—Needs

1. There should be an explanation to help the reader understand the acrostic poem. What does Harmony mean when she says *active, radio,* and *newspaper*?

2. Harmony started a mystery that the reader is to complete. But she did not set her writing up to be a mystery. Either she needs to revisit the mystery genre or she needs to recast this piece as a biography.

Multigenre Process—Strengths

1. Harmony took risks in using the birth announcement genre. She explored many birth announcements on the Internet.

2. Harmony was busy and used her writing time wisely.

3. Harmony worked with other students on revision and editing.

Multigenre Process—Needs

1. Harmony needed to seek support from fellow students and the teacher to expand her writing in her chosen genres.

2. Rather than leaving the mystery as it is currently written, she might have listened more closely to her revision conversations and expanded on this writing, as was suggested by other students and the teacher.

In viewing parts of Harmony's multigenre portfolio, it is clear what she understood and where she needed further support. She took risks with the announcement and poem, which were unfamiliar genres. However, each of these genres could still be expanded so that her knowledge could deepen. She also needed more instruction on what connotes a biography and a mystery. While revision is hard to see, her strengths as an editor do show. Her piece is almost perfect with respect to spelling, and she did an adequate job with punctuation and capitalization. Additionally, in the process of constructing her genres, she built an extensive knowledge base about Martin Luther King Jr.

Allison's Multigenre Portfolio

Allison chose a teacher as the topic for her multigenre project in the fifth grade. Her project began:

> I will not speak my name because my name is not important. It's what I do and have done that counts. I help children and parents all across the world. I work in a room with 1 to 100 students. My home away from home is school and giving people more knowledge is what I love and do. Hello, I am a teacher.

This introduction continued for four more pages, in which Allison detailed the education you need to become a teacher. She then discussed how important teachers are to all careers and how they must be role models and mentors for their students.

Allison made a variety of genre choices for her project. She included two letters, both written to the principal (see Figures 6.7 and 6.8). Her writing is very direct; she announces a problem and expects it to be solved. And in fact in the second letter, it is

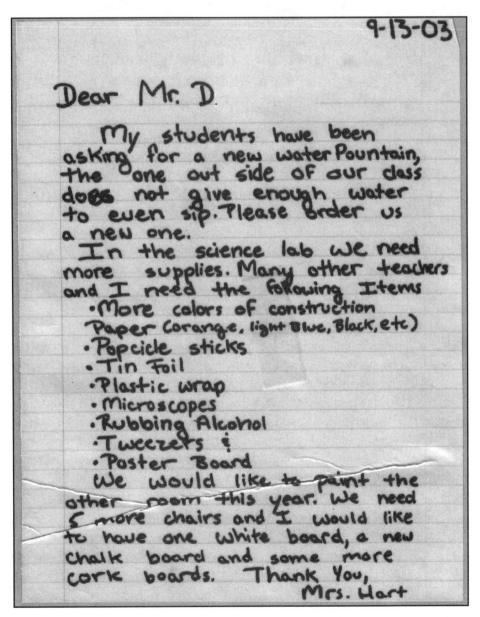

FIGURE 6.7
Allison's Letter to the Principal

FIGURE 6.8
Allison's Thank-You Letter

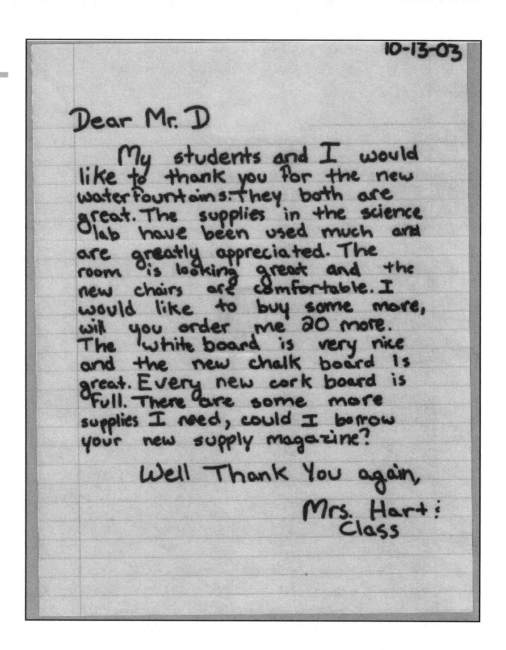

10-13-03

Dear Mr. D

My students and I would like to thank you for the new water fountains. They both are great. The supplies in the science lab have been used much and are greatly appreciated. The room is looking great and the new chairs are comfortable. I would like to buy some more, will you order me 20 more. The white board is very nice and the new chalk board is great. Every new cork board is full. There are some more supplies I need, could I borrow your new supply magazine?

Well Thank You again,

Mrs. Hart: Class

clear that the principal has repaired and purchased her items. However, we are left wondering if the principal will continue with this support now that she needs twenty more chairs and other supplies.

Her next writing genre is a substitute teacher schedule. She included information about teaching materials for the sub and an exact time line. Then she created bumper stickers: one about loving being a teacher and recruiting others to the profession and a second about the importance of parents reading to their children. Her final genre was several report cards for students in her class (see Figures 6.9, 6.10, and 6.11). We now revisit these genres and provide a possible evaluation scenario for them.

Multigenre Project—Strengths

1. The student completed four different genres around the topic of a teacher.

2. The pieces support each other and represent authentic artifacts used by teachers.

FIGURE 6.9
Allison's Substitute Teacher Schedule

Monday Schedule

8:00-8:35- Silent Reading
8:35- 9:10- Read <u>The Giver</u> to Class
9:10- 9:20- Have them read poetry
9:20-9:40- Recess (kids may stay in)
9:45- 10:30- Specials (ART) Get them at
10:35. (Back Door)
10:35-11:35-Math. Hand out sheet and
Mulitiplication. ← 2 min
11:35-12:35- Science. Have them read
pgs. 12-20 - if time do HO on pg. 21
12:35-12:40- Clean the room Completly!
12:40-1:30- Lunch and Recess (every one outs)
1:35-2:30-Writing. (multigenre projects)
2:30- 3:15- Social Studies
3:25- 3:35- Group disscussion
3:35- GO HOME (¨)

Thank You Very Much,
            Mrs. Hart

3. The project is neat and carefully edited.

4. Allison understood the genres of lesson plans, bumper stickers, letters, and report cards.

5. Her first letter to the principal could have been more persuasive in that she could have provided additional reasons for her material needs.

6. The project was turned in on time.

7. Visuals are interesting and the bumper stickers are appealing.

Multigenre Project—Needs

1. There are no defenses or reflections for the genres chosen. Allison needed to include these reflective pieces so that readers could better understand her choices.

2. Allison might have included a lesson plan rather than a schedule so that she could better show the planning that a teacher does.

FIGURE 6.10
Allison's Bumper Stickers

I ♥ MY TEACHER

Become A Teacher
Help Children Across
The World Learn

Teachers Inc.

Your Child Is A Great Student
Teachers Inc.

Be the best you can!
Teach Your child to
Read!!
Teachers Inc.

FIGURE 6.11
Allison's Report Card

Intermediate School

Student __Nancy__   Teacher __Mrs Hart__
Grade __6__   Year __2003__

Levels of Performance

4-Exceeds standards   3-Meets standards   2-Making progress to meet standards
1-Insufficient progress   0-Has not completed enough work

Writing

Writing Pieces:

Writing: Content and Mechanics

Writes for a variety of purposes	4
Narrows topic/subject	4
Uses descriptive language	4
Chooses topics that are meaningful	4
Writes with audience in mind	4+
Writes in paragraphs with a topic sentence	3

Revises for:

Word choice	3
Sentence structure	3+
Paragraph structure	3
Logical sequence	4
Self edits	3
Rewrites paper using revisions	3
Demonstrates effort in work	4
Turns assignments in on time	3

Comments: Nancy writes very interesting stories. I enjoy reading them

Grade: __A+__

Reading

Books Read:

Literature Logs and Discussions

Reads a variety of books	4
Analyzes books that are read	3
Participates in class discussion	3
Uses elements of literature taught	3
Explains feelings and impressions	4

Makes connections to:	
Other books	3
Own life	2
Similar themes and authors	3
Makes predictions	4
Confirms predictions	4
Demonstrates effort in work	4
Turns assignments in on time	4

Comments: Nancy has read 50 Books this semester.

Grade: __A+__ Great Ideas!

Spelling

Uses correct spelling:	
Written work	4+
Tests (percentage grade)	88%

Grade: __A__

Social Studies

Understands concepts covered in social Studies	3
Contributes to discussion and group activities	3
Demonstrates knowledge of geography	3
Demonstrates effort in work	3
Turns assignments in on time	4

Grade: __A+__

Multigenre Process—Strengths

1. Allison spent considerable amounts of time shadowing a teacher to learn about the roles and responsibilities.

2. Allison was continuously busy with writing during writing workshop.

3. Allison was always willing to work with other students and be a careful listener and responder.

Multigenre Process—Needs

1. Allison could have worked with other students on the revision and editing of the introduction to her teacher project. There were places that were redundant.

2. Allison needed to find time in the process to reflect on her genre choices.

Allison's multigenre project was much more detailed than Harmony's, although her reflections were not included. Her writing was more extensive and she included genres that are typical in teaching. The one major area that a teacher could respond to is improving her persuasive writing. It appears that Allison believes that if you make a request, it will be granted.

Julia's Multigenre Portfolio

The final multigenre project to be shared was created by a sixth-grade student, Julia. Her topic was being an engineer and in particular she chose Leonardo da Vinci as her model engineer. We chose her project because of the sophistication demonstrated within it. It allows teachers to see how a multigenre project supports the learning needs of even the most capable students. While Julia shared her defenses in a traditional font, all of her simulated da Vinci journal entries were written backward (they could be read when reflected in a mirror) to simulate the writing of da Vinci when he wrote important items. To facilitate the reading by others, she had copies with conventional print. Her genres included da Vinci's journal with entries from 1484 to 1519; an acceptance letter from a university, because that is the way to become an engineer; a college curriculum; a diploma; and a balloon speech with accompanying PowerPoint for an engineer (see Figures 6.12, 6.13, and 6.14.). Julia's balloon speech was quite long, so we share just a few snippets of it:

❖ A lot of people think that engineers are nerds with black glasses, white shirts, pocket protectors, and skinny black ties but that is so 1960. I'm an engineer and I stand before you as a human being who does the same things that the rest of the world does.

FIGURE 6.12
Julia's da Vinci Journal Entry

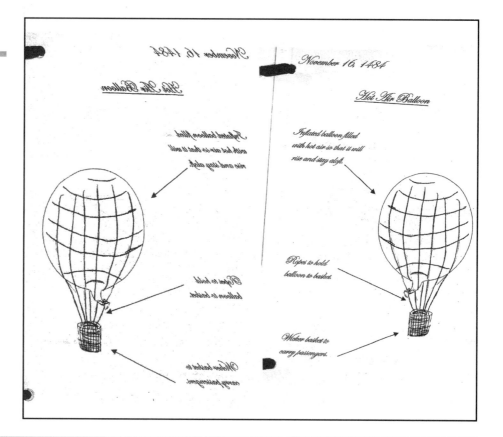

FIGURE 6.13
Julia's Curriculum Checklist

Curriculum Checklist
Mechanical Engineering

Degree Requirements: 127 credits
2.00 GPA in Engineering
4 Field Trips

Freshman Year

	Class	Credits
CO 150	Composition	3
M 169	Calculus for Physical Science I	4
M 161	Calculus for Physical Science II	4
ME 192	Intro. to Mechanical Engineering	2
ME 120	Intro. to Computer Aided Design	3
ME 121	Practicum	1
PH 141	Physics I	5
PH 142	Physics II	5
	Health and Wellness Elective	3
	Arts and Humanities Elective	3

Sophomore Year

	Class	Credits
C 111	General Chemistry I	4
C 112	General Chemistry Lab I	1
C 113	General Chemistry II	3
CE 260	Engineering Mechanics: Statics	3
CE 261	Engineering Mechanics: Dynamics	3
EE 204	Into. to Electrical Engineering	3
M 261	Calculus for Physical Science III	4
M 340	Intro. Ordinary Differential Equations	4
ME 237	Intro. Thermal Sciences	3
ME 250	Computer Application in Mechanical Engineering	2
ST 309	Statistics for Engineers and Scientists	3
	Communication Elective	3

FIGURE 6.14
Julia's Diploma

COLORADO STATE UNIVERSITY
upon the recommendation of the faculty of the
College of Engineering
has conferred the degree
Bachelor of Science in Mechanical Engineering
Summa Cum Laude upon
Julia Elizabeth
with all the honors, rights and privileges appertaining thereto.
In witness whereof, the seal of Colorado State University
and the proper signatures are hereunto affixed.
Given at Fort Collins, Colorado this seventeenth day of May, 2007, A.D.

Albert Einstein
Albert Einstein, Dean of the College of Engineering

Alfred Nobel
Alfred Nobel, President of the University

Benjamin Franklin
Benjamin Franklin, Chairman, Colorado Board of Regents

- The first engineers were the cavemen who first designed the wheel and tamed fire. Later engineers included Leonardo da Vinci, who came up with conceptual designs for the airplane and parachute way back in the 15th century.

- As Archimedes said, "Give me a big enough lever and a place to stand and I can move the world." Let's adopt the principles of the world's great engineers.

As we have done before, we invite you to consider the figures and participate in the evaluation process.

Multigenre Project—Strengths

1. The student completed five different genres around the topic of an engineer.

2. The pieces support each other and represent authentic artifacts used by da Vinci and students who are pursuing degrees in engineering.

3. The project is complete, well detailed, and completely edited.

4. Julia deeply understood how to write a journal and one in the style of da Vinci; her curriculum is for the entire degree program; her diploma looks authentic; her PowerPoint provides a rich background on engineers and what they do.

5. Her project demonstrates her multiple research endeavors on da Vinci, college programs, and diplomas.

6. Her reflections explain exactly why she included specific genres and why they were done as they were.

7. Sense of humor shows in balloon speech in introduction.

8. The project was turned in on time.

9. Visuals are interesting and complex, as seen in the journal entries.

Multigenre Project—Needs

1. Julia might explore other famous engineers to elaborate on da Vinci or to provide comparisons since she saw him as "one of the greatest minds of all times."

Multigenre Process—Strengths

1. Julia used the Internet to discover necessary research. When the classroom computer was being used, she went to the library. She also used her family's computer at home to extend her work.

2. Julia was continuously busy with writing during writing workshop.

3. Julia was always willing to work with other students and be a careful listener and responder.

Multigenre Process—Needs

1. None noted.

Julia used this project to gain information about engineers, university course work, and da Vinci. The depth of her knowledge showed in the careful crafting of da Vinci's journal. What isn't shown in the figures is that she included pieces of history and folklore pertinent to da Vinci's time and she wrote in his voice. For example, she wrote, "I hate to live in this era where my left-handedness is considered the devil's work," and "A few days ago my patron, Guiliano de' Medici passed away, but today practically made up for it. Today, King Francis I, himself, gave me the title of premier painter and engineer and architect to the king."

Her curriculum checklist demonstrates her care in finding out about coursework and credits for a degree in mechanical engineering. And teachers know that this can be a very difficult task even for graduate students, yet alone an elementary student. She also researched diplomas and created a very authentic-looking one for herself.

In her sharing of this project, she created a speech about engineers. She also created a PowerPoint where students had to simulate being engineers and work together to engineer a way off an island. She wrote, "We are on Island A and want to get to Island B. Hot air balloons can't fly in extreme weather and the trade winds in this area are extreme. If the wind isn't going in the right direction, we could become shark food." Through this simulation she moved beyond telling her audience about her discoveries to engaging them to behave as engineers and experience this profession.

Julia's project reveals how a student can expertly combine genres to create a whole that shares multiple facets of a topic. It demonstrates how a student can acquire expert knowledge so that her project, and in particular her journal, appears to be the authentic work of another person.

The three multigenre project portfolios display a wide range of student achievement, as documented in the final projects. We believe this to be a strength of these projects similar to the writing variations produced by students during writing workshop. While all students met the expectations of their projects (with the exception of reflections from Allison), they all did so with wide differences in their final products, especially as seen in their genre choices. Students were held responsible for certain parts of the project such as number of genres, when they were due, and so on. However, they made the choices of what, where, or who the topic would be and which genres would be the most appropriate. Through these decisions, they learned about genres, how to best write them to particular audiences, and the content related to their topics. And as with other writing projects, they developed their writing abilities through conferring with peers and their teachers about revision and editing needs.

Personal Reflections

As part of the multigenre project, students were asked to write a final retrospective reflection about the process and product. Teachers engaged in this process as well. The importance of this reflection was to consider the successes and challenges incurred during the project and to build from these through revision for the next multigenre project.

Student Reflections

Student reflections varied in quality and topic as did their projects. Following are several of these final reflections:

❖ I did my project because I thought that it would be a nice thing to do for my family and for me and for my cousins. My family is important to me and I thought it would be a nice thing for them to look at in the future.

❖ It was very fun to learn about Ruby Bridges because she was very brave to go through an angry mob.

❖ First of all, I have never done much non-fictional writing. In doing this multigenre project, I have not only learned about non-fictional characters but also improved my descriptive writing skills. When I choose from a variety of choices for my projects I learn to look for things like "How this fits into Susan B. Anthony's life" or "Why would this be something Susan would do?" Looking for these things, writing for different purposes, and describing why I chose a bumper sticker, pin, and diary, I learned to express feelings through my writing.

Each student self-reflection allows the student and teacher to see what was most important in this process. For the first student, it was about leaving memories of pleasant experiences for a family. For the next student, the content and personal connection to Ruby Bridges were the most important. And for the last student, learning to write and understanding the topic so well that the writer could think like Susan B. Anthony were the critical aspects of this writing. The reflections allow outsiders to understand the multiple meanings attached to multigenre projects.

Teacher Reflections

Importantly, teachers also stepped back from the process of multigenre writing and reflected to improve the next multigenre project. Suzette interviewed Ali at the end of her first experience with multigenre writing. Following are snippets from this interview:

ALI: Well, I think multigenre writing is still the way to be doing it. And I've been rethinking it a lot since this one. I think this one didn't go quite as well as I hoped. It was spread out too long, too much free time for some kids. Some kids handled it fine and came up with great projects. Kids who are struggling still struggled, other kids [who] were able to monitor and manage themselves did great with it.

SUZETTE: So why was it not, why didn't it work with the struggling writers?

ALI: I think it was too, the original time line that we set didn't work, it was too quick so then it got extended over break and then it got all the due dates messed up and then they lost their work and the more responsible students kept their stuff and knew what they were doing and knew where their drafts were. The kids who were struggling or more irresponsible lost their drafts and had to go back and redo their proposals.

SUZETTE: So it sounds as though organization was a bit difficult.

ALI: I think I overestimated the fact that it would get done quicker so my original organization plan didn't work and that's when stuff got lost.

SUZETTE: So even with the organization issues, what do you think about multigenre writing?

ALI: My biggest thing is that they're still excited about it.

SUZETTE: How do you organize to teach this project?

ALI: I think of what I want the end product to be and what that student can be taught along the way, decide if it's going to center on a topic such as the

American Revolution. If yes, then you have to give them lots of background information. If they are [going to] choose their own topic, it's a little bit different—you have to allow them the freedom to make good decisions [and make sure] that it's something they can actually write about and that the genres that they choose are going to work and fit with the topic.

SUZETTE: So how did choosing topics go?

ALI: Well, some of the topics they have chosen are pretty interesting. Some of them get a little bored by the end, but you know it's something they chose so they have ownership of it and they're excited to write. They see a cause and they see a purpose and they are excited. I think the kids are a little more interested when they are writing different genres.

ALI: The kids like it, they love it; they hound me every day about lack of writing time that they have so they, they're inspired to work. I don't think you see that as much in classrooms that don't use multigenre writing. These kids are pretty used to it now, but they're still fired up and excited.

SUZETTE: Do you think that there would be a difference in the way that you teach if your students had to take the state writing test?

ALI: I would probably do a test-writing genre at the beginning of the year and just teach it, who is your audience, it's the people who score [the] writing test and it's a different audience than a diary or something. So really looking for specific stuff, and how are we going to make our writing what that audience wants to read?

SUZETTE: Treating it as its own genre?

ALI: Yes, just as we teach reading for a test, reading comprehension questions as a genre, you know when you're reading a book for fun, you don't think the same way you do as when you know you have multiple-choice questions that you have to answer at the end. So, the same way that you read differently for test taking, you write differently for test taking.

During this interview, Ali first considered classroom management. She had issues with storage and time lines. Not surprisingly, classroom management issues surfaced first and fortunately are the easiest to repair. Next Ali talked about her students and how they enjoyed multigenre writing, although she was concerned about some of her struggling students. Unlike classroom management, this issue will take more thought about how to structure multigenre projects so that all students are fully involved. She may need to appoint partners for some children or she may need to have designated times during writing when certain students check in for progress monitoring.

At the end of the interview, Suzette asked directly about testing and if Ali would restructure her classroom for this assessment. Ali indicated that she would tweak her classroom curriculum a bit and share the genre of testing. Her approach makes sense, as a writing assessment is a genre in itself and needs to be explicitly taught. However, it does not need to consume a whole year's curriculum.

This chapter has taken a broad look at testing and standards and their relationship with multigenre writing. All of the evidence supports the claim that multigenre writing prepares students for these assessments and meets the expectations of national, state, and local standards. Moving from this view, we explored student multigenre projects to discover the variability of such projects and how they might be evaluated. Finally, we considered personal self-reflection that allowed a view into student learning and into how a teacher might reconsider a second or third foray into multigenre writing. All of the evidence documents the wealth of knowledge that students gain though multigenre writing—knowledge that supports them even when taking writing assessment tests.

References

Afflerbach, P. 2005. "National Reading Conference Policy Brief: High Stakes Testing and Reading Assessment." *Journal of Literacy Research* 37: 151–62.

Barone, D., and J. Taylor. 2006. *Improving Student Writing, K–8.* Thousand Oaks, CA: Corwin.

Calkins, L., K. Montgomery, D. Santman., and B. Falk. 1998. *A Teacher's Guide to Standardized Reading Tests: Knowledge Is Power.* Portsmouth, NH: Heinemann.

Cooper, J. 1997. *Literacy: Helping Children Construct Meaning.* Boston: Houghton Mifflin.

National Reading Panel. 2000. *Teaching Children to Read: An Evidence-Based Assessment of the Scientific Research Literature on Reading and Its Implications for Reading Instruction: Reports of the Subgroups.* Washington, DC: National Institute of Child Health and Human Development.

Shelton, N., and D. Fu. 2004. "Creating Space for Teaching Writing and for Test Preparation." *Language Arts* 82: 120–28.

Valencia, S. 1998. *Literacy Portfolios in Action.* Orlando, FL: Harcourt Brace College.

Valencia, S., and K. Wixson. 2001. "Inside English/Language Arts Standards: What's in a Grade?" *Reading Research Quarterly* 36: 2022–217.

CHAPTER 7

The Next Steps

Multigenre writing poses many possibilities for students to learn to read and write. It expands the boundaries of their learning as genres create layers of understanding for each individual writer. In our many years of teaching writing, students have asked over and over again for multigenre writing projects. It was from this enthusiasm that we wrote this book to help teachers embark on this exciting writing journey.

As we conclude, we envision teachers pondering ways of beginning multigenre writing with their students in appropriate ways for their classroom learning environment. We invite teachers to take a critical look at the purposes for writing and the importance of the selection of genre with their students. The power of genre instruction and multigenre writing opens avenues that help teachers create rich lessons and learning events that are embedded in authentic learning.

And we know that teachers may feel overwhelmed at the thought of bringing multigenre writing into their classrooms. To help alleviate this potential anxiety, we have crafted this chapter to respond to the question—Where should a teacher begin?

Establish the Writing Workshop

Before multigenre writing can be successful, we feel that the routine of a writing workshop needs to be in place. In Chapter 2 we discussed many ways for teachers to establish a predictable writing environment that supports students' writing efforts. There is no one right way to create a writing workshop, but it needs to be established from the first day of school so that students can depend on having that writing time and the predictability allows students to focus on writing rather than on guessing what is coming up next. Especially as multigenre writing begins, teachers need to feel that their students can be independent writers in order for the teacher to facilitate small-group investigations as well as one-on-one conferencing. The demands of multigenre writing on the teacher and students are great; therefore, the workshop needs to be well established so that students are comfortable with writing, reading, and discussing writing. Teachers seeking more information about writing workshops, might consider the following resources: *The Writing Workshop* by Katie Wood Ray (2001), *The Writing Workshop* by Ralph Fletcher and Joanne Portalupi (2001), and *Writing K–8* by Diane Barone and Joan Taylor (2006). These are great books to help establish routines, develop curriculum, and understand the nature of more directed instruction in the writing workshop.

Establish Literary Discussions of Texts and Focus on Genre

Just as important as the routine and expectations of the writing workshop is the routine and practice of critical conversations about literature. These conversations become important as students investigate genre and discuss the importance and effectiveness of each genre example. During the reading workshop, students question and think critically about the literature they are reading. Teachers can facilitate this kind of literary knowledge through the use of read-alouds, think-alouds, and literature discussion groups. Through these practices, students and teachers share their insights about literature and develop a community of readers.

As students become more proficient and comfortable with discussing their personal reactions to texts and are engaged in the discussion process, the teacher can then help children move to an evaluative stage where they begin to analyze and interpret the literature being read. Students and teachers begin to ask: Who is writing it? Who is the audience? What purpose does the genre have? What point of view is it written in? Is it effective? What if you changed this perspective? How do I personally connect to the book? What literary connections can I make? and Why would someone write this? Those practices established in the reading workshop help students develop an interpretive repertoire, which supports students in evaluating the genres they wish to emulate.

Some resources to help with the generation of these conversations are *Grand Conversations,* by Ralph Peterson and Maryann Eeds (1990), *Tell Me,* by Aiden Chambers (1996), *Interpreting Literature with Children,* by Shelby A. Wolf (2004), and *Around the Reading Workshop in 180 Days,* by Frank Serafini and Suzette Serafini Youngs (2006).

Establish a Connection Between Reading and Writing

Once the writing workshop is in place and children are discussing and interpreting literature in whole-class and small-group discussions and through individual literature response logs, it seems natural to make a closer connection between reading and writing. As teachers read particular genres in class, or explore thematic units of study, students begin to explore this kind of writing. Throughout this book we have highlighted many aspects of reading and writing instruction, and it is evident how multigenre writing creates an intricate connection between reading and writing. In order for students to write from a particular perspective, they must understand the genres that are available to them to communicate most effectively.

As this talk about texts and genres develops, teachers can utilize this understanding to make the transition from reading like a writer to writing like a reader. As writers make this shift, they understand the purposes for writing and the power of particular genres and can therefore transfer this knowledge into their multigenre writing projects.

There should be a close connection between what students read and what they write. It would be expected that teachers and students read and share multiple genres so that ongoing discoveries are made of new possibilities for genres.

Utilize Existing Units Within the Curriculum

As described before, Suzette began with a unit of study that already existed in her curriculum and then added multigenre writing as a way to expand students' knowledge about a particular historical figure. This might be a way for some teachers to add multigenre writing to an already crowded curriculum. A social studies topic makes a great foundation for a multigenre writing project, as it is a way to combine history and literacy as students read across the content areas. As a culminating project teachers can request that students choose topics of interest to further their understanding of an historical concept and express their understanding of a topic through multigenre writing or to demonstrate proficiency in an area the teacher expects them to understand.

When teachers utilize units of study that are familiar because they are parts of their existing curriculum, they already understand genres that are prominent within the topic and can help children navigate possible writing topics and genres. As teachers become familiar with multigenre writing, they will eventually expand these early writing projects so students research their own topics of interest and replace or add on to the research paper or report, a standard genre in most writing curricula.

Begin with a Small Project or Whole-Class Project

Another option for exploring multigenre writing is to use a piece of literature like *Voices in the Park* (Browne 2001) and have students create multigenre writing pieces written to or from the main characters to create a book much like *The Jolly Postman, or, Other People's Letters* (Ahlberg and Ahlberg 2001). Teachers and students discuss the nature of genre and how genres are effective for particular people and situations. The students can create a class book and put all the genres together to form one multigenre writing project.

Yet another way is to have all the students create a writing piece on a particular unit of study and to have each student write through a different genre. When the pieces are completed, again create a class book, or rather a multigenre writing project on one central topic. As a class project the research can be controlled and every student can read the same material or students could each study something different about a topic and utilize particular genres that would make sense to their research efforts.

In either of these examples, teachers use the curriculum expectations yet they are able to explore the study of genre. This also allows teachers to enter into the concept of multigenre writing without having to navigate the complex structure of the individual multigenre projects described in Chapters 4 and 5. We encourage teachers to explore the possibilities of writing and learning through different genres. As children try on different perspectives, their writing takes on a creative elegance and children find powerful and meaningful perspectives to express their research interests.

Envision Possibilities for Struggling Writers

One question that always is asked is how to help the struggling writer not to become overwhelmed with the management and organization of multigenre writing and to stay focused with so many pieces of writing to attend to. We think that for those writers, teachers will want to work with them one on one every day in a small-group or individual setting to help create small daily writing goals that are clearly attainable. Some writers give up once they realize the number of writing pieces that are expected of them. In this case teachers need to make this project accessible. By working with them every day to set short-term goals, teachers can help them reach daily accomplishments. For some writers it might be necessary to have them focus on only one writing piece at a time and not worry about other pieces; in fact, they might propose only one at a time. In this manner students focus on one piece and do not feel overwhelmed, and then the teacher can tailor the reading and writing to each particular student's needs.

On the other hand the great aspect of multigenre writing is the flexibility with the writing pieces, and so those students who get bored or lose focus quickly can opt to begin another piece and return to earlier writing pieces when they feel inspired. It will still require a lot of scaffolding on the part of the teacher to help students understand each genre and the writing possibilities for it, but it gives a writer the OK to shift from one piece of writing to another, often discovering new ways to enhance a text's meaning.

Create Connections Between Home and School

Teaching and learning that focus on genre also bridge the gap of school and home. As students begin to investigate topics and genres, they are able to demonstrate proficiency with school-based genres such as narrative writing and informational reports. Students combine these basic genres with those that may be more personally relevant to them such as banners, emails, and notes. In this way children create a rich project that is meaningful to them and satisfies school expectations. We think one of the benefits of the multigenre writing project is that students learn to write in many genres. If the standards mandate that students write a narrative or a report, it can be one required element within the project and then students can choose four or five other genres that are not typically taught or used in the school setting. This flexibility gives choice and power to the student and yet helps the teacher meet curricular demands.

Create Your Own Multigenre Writing Project

We think one of the best ways to begin to understand multigenre writing projects is to actually create one. As a teacher chooses particular topics and genres to articulate the essence of the topic, or rather a layered understanding of the topic, he will come to understand the concept of multigenre writing as a writer. This writing process will allow teachers an inside view into the complexities and possibilities that a multigenre focus can bring to a topic of study. Teachers will also be able to use the project as an example, thus sharing insights on how to complete one and struggles of writing as well. We recommend that teachers create one during summer months when they have time to spend on research and writing.

In addition teachers will want to write in front of students because the end project does not show *how* a teacher put the project together and the only way to demonstrate that is to create one *with* your students, so they can hear about the decisions. An easy way to manage this is to continue to use the topic from the project created in the summer months to demonstrate various phases of the writing process in front of students. In this manner the research is completed, the teacher has a model to show students, yet the topic is rich enough to support further writing that can be completed in front of or with the students.

Reflections on Multigenre Writing

Students have always been eager to share the genres they discovered. They also enjoy the variety of stances toward writing as they investigate one topic but use many avenues to express ideas on a topic. We have enjoyed the challenge of helping children investigate and define a particular genre as we learned about genres at the same time. It is wonderful to watch children of all ability levels find genres that fit their conceptual framework; they become better writers as they select genres that scaffold them to the next level of learning.

In this book we shared our units of study and our vision for multigenre writing. Students have told us they enjoy the freedom of topic and genres and like the creativity that comes with discovering new and unique genres. We have also documented their growth as writers through this process. We end the book with a quote from Anna's reflections on multigenre writing, in which she identifies a student's view of the importance of multigenre writing:

> I would recommend it to kids in other classrooms cuz I think it is a way to expand one topic into four different genres and you could do more if you had time and you can get ideas from your class and you just keep on improving. I think it is a way to improve your writing cuz you have time to go through each project.
>
> Sometimes when the teacher picks the topic it's hard to live with. Multigenre writing is basically you get to choose your own topic and you get to choose whatever genre you want and it is a way for classmates and your teacher to know what you like and how you are writing. If you're doing a topic that you don't know a lot about then it teaches you and you learn more about your topic

and you find out new perspectives. It is a fun project and you could be really creative so you can have fun with it. Writing about anything, really it doesn't feel like a homework kind of thing—it feels like free time kind of thing that you would really want to do.

References

Ahlberg, J. and A. Ahlberg. 2001. *The Jolly Postman, or, Other People's Letters.* New York: Little, Brown.

Barone, D., and J. Taylor. 2006. *Writing K–8.* Thousand Oaks, CA: Corwin.

Browne, A. 2001. *Voices in the Park.* New York: DK.

Chambers, A. 1996. *Tell Me: Children, Reading, and Talk.* York, ME: Stenhouse.

Fletcher, R., and J. Portalupi. 2001. *The Writing Workshop: The Essential Guide.* Portsmouth, NH: Heinemann.

Graves, D. 1994. *A Fresh Look at Writing.* Portsmouth, NH: Heinemann.

Peterson, R., and M. Eeds. 1990. *Grand Conversations: Literature Groups in Action.* New York: Scholastic.

Serafini, F., and S. Serafini Youngs. 2006. *Around the Reading Workshop in 180 Days: A Month-by-Month Guide to Effective Instruction.* Portsmouth, NH: Heinemann.

Wolf, S. 2004. *Interpreting Literature with Children.* Mahwah, NJ: Lawrence Erlbaum.

Wood Ray, K. 2001. *The Writing Workshop: Working Through the Hard Parts (And They're All Hard Parts).* Urbana, IL: NCTE.

Grand Canyon Children's Literature Selections

Anderson, P. 1997. *A Grand Canyon Journey: Tracing Time in Stone*. London: Franklin Watts.

Christian, S., and A. Felix. 1998. *What Makes the Grand Canyon Grand? The World's Most Awe-Inspiring Natural Wonders*. San Francisco: Jossey-Bass.

Foster, L. 1990. *Exploring the Grand Canyon*. Grand Canyon: Grand Canyon Association.

Hall, M. 2005. *Grand Canyon National Park*. Portsmouth, NH: Heinemann

Henry, M. 1981. *Brighty of the Grand Canyon*. New York: Aladdin.

Justesen, W., and J. Newhouse. 2005 *"Hey Ranger!" Kids Ask Questions About Grand Canyon National Park*. San Ramon, CA: Falcon.

Mihesuah, D. 2004. *Grand Canyon Rescue: A Tuli Black Wolf Adventure*. Bangor, ME: Booklocker.

Minor, W. 1998. *Grand Canyon: Exploring a Natural Wonder*. Troy, MI: Blue Sky.

Skurzynski, G., and A. Ferguson. 2002. *Over the Edge: Mysteries in Our National Parks*. Washington, DC: National Geographic Children's.

Trumbauer, L. 2005. *Grand Canyon*. Danbury, CT: Children's Press.

Vieira, L. 2000. *Grand Canyon: A Trail Through Time*. New York: Walker.

Revolutionary War Children's Literature Selections

Picture Books

Marzollo, J. 1994. *In 1776*. New York: Scholastic.

Krensky, S. 2002. *Paul Revere's Midnight Ride*. New York: HarperCollins.

Swoboda Lunn, J. L. 1998. *Charlotte*. Toronto: Tundra Books.

Kirkpatrick, K. 1999. *Redcoats and Petticoats*. New York: Holiday House.

Turner, A. W. 1992. *Katie's Trunk*. New York: Aladdin.

Rockwell, A. 2002. *They Called Her Molly Pitcher*. New York: Knopf.

Fritz, J. 1997. *Can't You Make Them Behave, King George?* New York: Coward, McCann and Geoghegan.

Peacock, L. 1998. *Crossing the Delaware: History in Many Voices*. New York: Scholastic.

Berieth, R. 1990. *Samuel's Choice*. Morton Grove, IL: Albert Whitman.

Chapter Books

Reit, S. 1990. *Guns for General Washington: A Story of the American Revolution*. New York: Harcourt.

Woodruff, E. 1991. *George Washington's Socks*. New York: Scholastic.

McGovern, A. 1990. *The Secret Soldier: The Story of Deborah Sampson*. New York: Scholastic.

Avi. 1984. *The Fighting Ground*. New York: HarperTrophy.

Brady, E. W. 1993. *Toliver's Secret*. New York: Yearling.

Van Wyck, M. 1978. *Winter at Valley Forge*. New York: Random House.

Quackenbush, J. 1999. *Daughters of Liberty*. New York: Hyperion.

Kroll, S. 1998. *Boston Tea Party*. New York: Holiday House.

Building Community Focus Unit Literature Selections

Browne, A. 1986. *Piggybook.* New York: Alfred A. Knopf.

———. 2001. *Voices in the Park.* New York: DK.

Egan, J. 1996. *Metropolitian Cow.* Boston: Houghton Mifflin.

Fox, M. 1992. *Tough Boris.* San Diego, CA: Harcourt Brace.

———. 1997. *The Straight Line Wonder.* New York: Mondo.

Henkes, K. 1991. *Chrysanthemum.* New York: Greenwillow.

Howe, J. 1999. *Horace and Morris but Mostly Dolores.* New York: Atheneum Books for Young Readers.

Hughes, L. 1996. *The Dream Keeper and Other Poems.* New York: Knopf Books for Young Readers.

Konigsburg, E. L. 1996. *The View from Saturday.* New York: Simon and Schuster.

Lester, H. 1988. *Tacky the Penguin.* New York: Houghton Mifflin.

Martin, R. 1992. *The Rough-Face Girl.* New York: Puffin.

Rahaman, V. 1997. *Read for Me, Mama.* New York: Boyds Mills.

Say, A. 1999. *Tea with Milk.* New York: Houghton Mifflin.

Sendak, M. 1963. *Where the Wild Things Are.* New York: Harper and Row.

Zolotow, C. 1972. *William's Doll.* New York: Harper and Row.

Index